Averin's Letters from Bangkok

Diary of a British Embassy wife, Part 1: 1957

With a Foreword and Notes by

Michael Richard Hinton

orrydian

Contents

Foreword

by Michael Richard Hinton

Averin and Geoffrey in St Albans, spring 1957

Averin Macalister married Geoffrey Hinton in Bourton-on-the-Water in Gloucestershire in 1942. During World War II Geoffrey was an intelligence officer working in Egypt, Palestine and Greece. After the war he continued working for SIS, the Secret Intelligence Service, otherwise known as MI6, as station commander in Cairo, with attachment to the British Embassy as 3rd Secretary providing cover for his intelligence role. Averin accompanied him to Cairo, and my younger sister and I were born there during this period. In 1952 the family moved back to England and settled in St Albans. Geoffrey worked in London until 1957, when he was posted to Bangkok to take over as station commander there, again with attachment to the British Embassy and the rank of 1st secretary as cover. He and my mother, Averin, were in Bangkok from May 1957 until March 1961, while my sisters and I were farmed out to different boarding schools in England and to various kind relatives who took care of us during the school holidays. We three children made two visits to

Bangkok, in the summer holidays of 1958 and 1960.

Throughout the posting, Averin wrote round-robin letters to the family back in England, and most of these letters have survived. They were typed and carbon-copied, and occasionally Averin added personal hand-written notes. Most of the handwritten notes in my collection were to Averin's sister Margaret, my Aunt Margaret, who acted as my guardian for these four years.

Averin had herself worked for SIS for a short time during the war. Like Geoffrey, she was bound by the Official Secrets Act, and so, frustratingly, there is no hint at all in any of the letters as to Geoffrey's real role. And it wasn't until the early 1970s that my sisters and I learnt that he was working for MI6 rather than the Diplomatic Service.

This volume, Part 1, contains the letters dated May to December 1957.

The family

These family members are referred to in the letters.

Averin Hinton, born 1921 in Liverpool. Married to Geoffrey. Sometimes referred to as *A*.

Geoffrey Hinton, born 1918 in Reading. Married to Averin. Sometimes referred to as *G* or *Geoff.*

Ann, **Michael** and **Jill**, Averin and Geoffrey's chidren.

Leslie Macalister, Averin's mother and guardian of Ann and Jill during this period. Referred to as *Leslie* or *Granny* or *Mummy.*

C. J. Macalister, Averin's father, died in 1943.

F. J. Hinton, Geoffrey's father. Official name John, but known in the family as *Dai* or *Gran'pa.*

Florence Hinton, Geoffrey's step-mother, married to Dai. Referred to as *Florence* or *Auntie Gran.*

Margaret Stephen, Averin's elder sister and Michael's guardian.

Stuart Stephen, Margaret's husband.

Ian, **Carolyn** and **Vanessa**, Margaret and Stuart's children.

Sheila Rippon, one of Averin's half-siblings, children of C. J. Macalister's first marriage.

25th May: "There is almost nobody la-di-dah"

NOTES

On 10th May 1957 Averin and Geoffrey sailed from Southampton, travelling 1st class on the Dutch ship m.s. Oranje to Singapore, where Geoffrey had some work to do. After a few days there they flew on to Bangkok. This is a handwritten letter on the ship's headed notepaper to Margaret, Averin's sister.

1950s poster

m.s. "ORANJE"
May 25th, 1957

My dear Margaret,

We got a letter from Geoff's father yesterday saying that Michael seemed to be doing all the right things at school. He'd also had letters from all sorts of people (including you) who never dreamed of writing to him before, so he's probably doing much better than he would if we were still at home!

We're having a very good trip, as these things go, but I for one shall be glad when it comes to an end. It gets rather monotonous being in a state of perpetual holiday. We had rather a rough time in the Bay of Biscay and I was both astonished and pained to find myself being seasick there. However, the Mediterranean sea was perfect, warm and sunbathey, and we sailed fairly close to the coast of North Africa so there was something to look at most of the time. At Port Said the British, Australians, French and Israelis weren't allowed to go ashore but that didn't worry us, and anyway lots of little boats came out to the ship's side with things to sell, and some Egyptians even set up shop on board, and business was still going strong long past midnight when we went to bed, so we missed nothing except for a leg-stretch ashore.

We caused quite a lot of excitement in the Suez Canal because we were one of the first ships through after the political situation. The Egyptian rich cruised along in their American cars beside us, tapping out welcoming tattoes on their klaxons, while the poor left their goats or their slumbers or whatever it was and rushed to the water-edge to cheer us. Of course we were a Dutch ship, but I don't think they would have been hostile if we had been British

Then came Aden which was intolerably stinky hot, and those of us who went on shore returned after an hour completely exhausted, our faces bedewed with sweat and our clothes sodden with the same. Even the natives were obviously not enjoying it, and one told us bitterly that this was only the beginning of the hot season. The Red Sea was also hot, with not a breath of air to soothe us, and my only comfort was to get into the swimming pool and stay there as long as possible. The water in it, straight from the sea, and always flowing through, is never cooler than 86° F, but its saltness and wetness have a refreshing effect. We were promised that the Indian Ocean would be cooler than the Red Sea but something has gone wrong with the weather (I thought this only happened in England) and it was just as hot. Our cabin is very sticky and restless at night. Some have air-conditioning and our table-mates, for instance, come to breakfast every morning saying how cool & refreshed they've been and how they needed one blanket. Ours is very high up, above the promenade deck, and it has windows that open, presumably to let the air in, but as the air is hot and humid it doesn't do much good.

Yesterday we stopped in Colombo for six hours. The monsoons had just started and it poured with torrential rain, and natives went about with black umbrellas and schoolgirls, dressed in prim white dresses, took off their shoes and paddled home. We went on a Cook's bus tour round the city and were permitted to see over a Dutch church and a Buddhist temple. We also saw a snake charmer who charmed his snake and did some gully-gully tricks for a consideration. We arrive in Singapore on the 28th and will be staying there for at least a week as Geoffrey has some work to do.

We're having a very luxurious time on board. The 1st Class consists almost entirely of people like ourselves whose passage is paid by their employers as a matter of prestige, so there is almost nobody la-di-dah, either Dutch or British. There are Lancashire accents and West Country accents, South African accents, Scottish accents, and a few B.B.C. Everybody dresses nicely of course, but then we've all been given clothing allowances as part of the prestige. The food is full of steaks and turkey and pheasant and such undreamed of debaucheries and we have a dance or a film or something every evening. Sunday evenings seem to be reserved for simple, communal gambling games, which offend some Presbyterian conscience within me, but I play them nevertheless. All notices are given out in English as well as Dutch and there is a good English fiction library, so we British feel quite at home and need hardly notice the existence of other nationalities!

Goodness knows when I shall write again. You'll let us know, *won't you, when you need more money for Michael?*

Much love to all of you - Averin, & from Geoff

N.V. STOOMVAART MAATSCHAPPIJ "NEDERLAND" — AMSTERDAM

NOTES

The Gully Gully Man was a magician that visited ships to entertain the passengers, particularly in the River Nile, the Suez Canal and round the coast of Africa.

30th May: "I shall be glad when we get to Bangkok"

[Postcard from Averin to Michael. Averin and Geoffrey were in Singapore for a few days before flying on to Bangkok. Transcription:]

Railway Station SEREMBAN
Seremban is the capital of the State of Negri Sembilan.

Singapore May 30, 1957
I must confess I haven't seen a Singapore train yet and I don't suppose I shall before we leave by air at squeak of dawn tomorrow morning. The man on the left of this picture is riding a bicycle with a sort of chair on wheels attached to it. There are many of these about and I suppose you might call them the poor man's taxi. We got the letter you wrote to Cape Town on May 12th yesterday. All our mail from England is topsey-turvey and I shall be glad when we get to Bangkok and it straightens itself out.

Love from Mummy.

NOTES

The "bicycle with a sort of chair on wheels" mentioned in this postcard is known in Thailand as a samlor. It is not possible to include the postcard picture for copyright reasons.

1st June: "Like stepping into an oven"

FIRST IMPRESSIONS OF BANGKOK, JUNE 1st 1957

We flew from Singapore starting early in the morning. The plane was a Super-Constellation of QANTAS Airways, first class only, travelling through to London, and many passengers were wearing warm suits or coats and skirts in spite of the heat. I was wearing a cotton dress and felt quite hot enough in that.

We flew at 16,000 feet and could see the Malayan jungle beneath us - a massive carpet of green treetops. Then we were over the sea which was sky-blue with little puffs of white clouds here and there. It seemed no time at all before we were in sight of land again - Thailand, this time. Here the sky was clouded over in places and there was evidence of storms. We passed low over Bangkok and could see the lines of klongs and traffic busy in the streets. Then we were coming down to land at the airport; the journey had taken 3½ hours.

We had been told that getting out of the plane would be like stepping into an oven, but we could see by the pools of water on the tarmac that there had been recent rain and it wasn't unpleasantly hot at all. Ellis was waiting to meet us and as soon as we had been through the customs we got into his car and drove off. After the dry, dusty weather the first rains had made the road treacherously slippery so we crawled along slowly.

"How many cars in this klong?" Ellis asked his driver. He was delighted to hear that there were three, and indeed we saw them, looking very dismal with water over their door-handles.

We passed through paddy fields and villages with huts on stilts and naked children playing around them. Modesty seemed more important for girls than for boys for little girls frequently wore minute aprons tied round the waist with string. There were higher class houses too, built in pleasant modern style and one very large building with a green roof.

Then we were in the busy streets where women carried great burdens slung from flat, supple poles carried over one shoulder and men and women worked together at road repairs. They wore coolie hats of straw, some conical and some rounded on top, to protect them from the heat. As in all Eastern towns the shops were open and their wares stacked out on the pavement for all to see. They were grouped together according to the wares they sold. Hence there were the goldsmiths' shops, sometimes four or five in succession, with impressive glass counters and a wealthy array of golden objects behind plate glass at the back of the shop. The silversmiths protect their ware behind glass too, but in what might be called "Material Lane" shop after shop spilled out stacks of different-coloured materials to attract the passer-by.

In the streets themselves the samlors took up a good deal of room and looked as if they were asking to be smashed up by passing cars, but we learned later that in all circumstances the samlor has right of way and a car-driver involved in an accident with one is almost certain to be in the wrong.

Aamlor-filled street in the 1950s

The samlor is a tricycle with a wide, shaded seat between the two back wheels. It carries the yellow number-plate of the hired vehicle and is owned by its driver, who is completely content to earn his living in this independent way. He usually wears a navy blue cotton shirt and shorts and a straw hat and nothing on his feet. If he is very wealthy he drives a motor-bike samlor but the pedal cycle is more usual. The streets were heavy with cars of every description, large and small. Traffic was risk-taking but fairly orderly.

We were thankful at last to find ourselves in a more residential area. At last we turned right into a lane by a Mobiloil service station: Soi Lang Suan, the lane was called and it was pleasantly overhung with trees, with a khlong on one side and a green hedge on the other. We turned into the drive of no. 46, and there we were, home at last, looking at a white teak house with overhanging eaves and verandahs shaded by trellised creeper.

The Hintons' house at 46 Soi Lang Suan, Bangkok

NOTES

Ellis, who met Averin and Geoffrey at the airport, may have been Dick Ellis, who had been MI6's "controller Far East" until 1953.

5th June: "We seem to have six servants"

British Embassy,
Bangkok.

June 5th, 1957

Dear Everybody,

Forgive me if I write to you all like this, but there are so many things to tell about and I couldn't bear to have to write it out several times over! I expect there'll be rather a gap between this letter and the last ones we sent from Singapore. The bag leaves here on Fridays and as we arrived on a Saturday we had to wait six days before we could send anything. I advise you not to use the bag address but to carry on with the air-letters because bag from England goes by sea and takes at least five weeks. On the other hand if we send airmail letters they're apt to be stolen for the stamps, I'm told.

On our last night in Singapore we were invited to a cocktail party and then taken out to dinner and then went to visit some friends on a French ship which was in port for 24 hours. So we got to bed at 1 a.m. and at 5 a.m. we were up again, ready for an early start. We were driven out to the airport in torrential rain and then had to wait minutes while a windscreen wiper was mended on the plane, which was a super-constellation of QANTAS Airlines (Australian). Very super it was too: all first-class, a charming air-hostess, a steward who brought us tea and sausage-rolls at 10 o'clock and a skipper who told us all we wanted to know.

We didn't fly very high - about 16,000 feet - so we could see the Malayan jungle rolling away beneath us, and then we were over the sea which was so blue that it looked like the sky, especially as there were a few puffy white clouds floating about beneath us. Then it seemed no time before we were coming down over Bangkok. The airport is about 20 miles from the city. We were met by a F.O. friend and everything went very smoothly and we were soon in our own house.

I find this rather difficult to describe from the outside. It's rather dirty white with an overhanging roof to keep off the sun and rain. There's a lot of foliage draped over the verandahs and a lot - yes, a great many - of open windows, although you can't really call them windows because there's no glass in most of them. They're just holes which can be covered by shutters if required. The garden is perhaps a little bigger than the 9, Avenue Road one, only the house is bang in the middle of it, and at the back there is an assortment of very respectable little wooden houses where the servants live with their families. The garden at the back of the house always seems to be full of little sunburned children who yap-yap-yap away in Siamese, and a great many people seem to come and go who have nothing to do with us at all.

Inside, the house is very pleasant. It's old, which is why it looks rather drab from the outside, but inside it has quite a lot of character. All the walls are of white painted wood, and the whole of the ground floor is all in one piece, with a dining recess, a vague middle recess with a few cupboards round the walls, and then the sitting-room recess which is about three times the size of the drawing-room at number 9. It's all very nicely furnished and there are a few odd mats and a carpet which aren't really necessary but look agreeable. Downstairs, also, there is a small study which can be shut off from the rest, and a pantry and a bathroom. The cookhouse and the wash-house are separate little buildings out at the back. I haven't yet discovered how food is brought in when it's pouring with rain! Oh, yes, and there's an enormous refrigerator which almost has a small room (well, an alcove, anyway) to itself.

Upstairs there are three bedrooms and a bathroom-cum-lav. The plug of the latter is by way of pulling but water pressure is low and we are apt to find ourselves replenishing the tank with water out of a sort of ali-baba earthenware jar, scooped up with an old saucepan, and then pulling. A lot of water gets sloshed over the floor during this operation but this is a matter of small importance. (The ali-baba jar stands in the bathroom and we imagine it must be there for just this purpose).

Our bedroom is the smallest of the lot. This is because it has air-conditioning, which really gives us deliciously cool nights. The other two bedrooms have ceiling fans. One has two beds and the other (attention, children!) three. This big one has french windows leading onto an enormous balcony which is cool and shaded-over and I imagine that one could mess about there happily for hours.

We seem to have six servants, which if course sounds ridiculous, but doesn't seem quite so ridiculous when you're living with them. There's an old Chinese cook, a man, who is such a good cook that various people tried to steal him while the house was empty but he wouldn't go for some reason, and we're very glad about this. He sets off to market every morning in a samlore, a sort of large tricycle with a shaded, comfortable seat supported between the two back wheels, and for this transport we have to pay 2 ticals (about 8d) daily. He has five or six gold upper front teeth, but no other teeth that I can see. I'm told that to have gold teeth is a way of saving for your old age. When you need money you have a tooth taken out and sell the gold. This is certainly safer than keeping your savings in a stocking, like some people do in England.

Then there is a mother and her daughter who call themselves coolie and number one boy. The coolie is supposed to do the donkey work in the house and the number one boy hands out drinks (a prominent feature in Far Eastern social life) or waits at table. In fact, these two do the donkey work and the other things together. The girl is only fourteen and her mother wants her trained as a number one boy. Her name is Saam-See (you pronounce it as if you are asking two questions: Saam? See?) and she's a nice bright, cheerful little girl and is doing her best to learn

English. We pay her and her mother together as if they were one good servant (which, in fact, together, they are.)

Som See and Chai, No.1 boy and her mother

Every morning at 8.30 the wash-amah arrives. She is a middle-aged, wizened woman whom I supply with sunlight soap and FAB (a sort of DAZ) and a great bag of starch, and charcoal (for heating water and also her own special iron). She then washes and irons EVERYTHING, from the smallest underclo' to the largest sheet. Dresses and shirts are beautifully starched and Geoff's tropical suits look as if they've been done by a professional. Sometimes the two of us don't give her too much work to do, but I think she brings some of her own washing along as well and does our Cookie's washing too. Our clothes don't get very dirty but they do get sweaty and we change underclothes at least once during the day. The gardener is a handsome, smiling lad who seems to be busy doing something all day, and finally there is the driver who drives Geoff to work every morning and takes me shopping or visiting if I have shopping or visiting to do. You must understand here that it's really too hot to walk anywhere during the day so everybody has a car or the use of one. The Siamese, of course, walk, but then they're used to the heat. The driver and his wife look very young but I think most of the children who play in the garden belong to them.

Suk the gardener in front of the servants' house

One of the first to welcome us 'home' was a dog, a native of this country, who has attached himself to the house and adopts gratefully anyone who comes to live in it. He's a clean, well-fed, friendly fellow, who comes in and out as he pleases and makes a squeaky fuss of you or ignores you as he chooses. I have also seen a cat, which looked the other way when I approached. At this moment there is a cockroach running about at top speed all over the typewriter. I hope he won't get into the works and die a squashy death. (I bet that made you squeal, Auntie Gran!) I haven't told you everything, of course, but you'll be getting bored if I go on so I'll wait and inflict another scroll on you all next week.

Much love, Averin

NOTES

9 Avenue Road was the house in St Albans that the Hintons rented from 1952-1957.

Auntie Gran was Florence Hinton, Geoffrey's step-mother, married to his father Dai.

11th June: "A very hectic first week"

46 Lang Suan Lane,
Bangkok.

June 11th, 1957

Dear Everybody,

I didn't tell you how hot it is in my last letter. Well, it is hot! However, we've missed something because people say they've been having the worst summer for 20 years, and that's all finished now because the rains have started, but if you imagine it rains solidly all the time you're wrong because some days it doesn't rain at all and most days there's just one (or perhaps two) torrential showers. I gather the rains gather momentum as the weeks go by and July and August are very wet indeed and outside Bangkok some of the roads get washed away and inside the road-surfaces get very bumpy.

It's the stickiness of the heat that's so uncomfortable. You get sweaty and because of the humidity in the air the sweat doesn't dry off you so you get wet all over. I went with a friend to do some sight-seeing yesterday and after two hours our one thought was to dash home and have a cold shower and change every garment we had on. It doesn't get much cooler at night so we sit in the evening with all the windows open and the mosquitoes fly in and eat us up. They just love our fresh, rich English blood and my arms and legs are one big itch. There's some stuff called sketolene which is supposed to keep them away and I lavish this upon my person but the mosquitoes don't seem to realise that it's supposed to be a signal for them to lay off. Geoff isn't in such a bad way because he wears more clothes, but he too does quite a lot of scratching.

The embassy here consists of a compound with about five

large, white, dignified buildings, all about the same size and arranged symmetrically (our heavy luggage hasn't arrived yet so I can't consult the dictionary about whether that's spelt properly), two in front and two immediately behind and one (the Ambassador's house) in the middle at the back. The others, I think, are chancery (where Geoff works), the consulate, the counsellor's house and the head of chancery's house. Attached to chancery there is a shop where you can buy certain foods, like butter and cheese and tinned stuff, more cheaply than in the Bangkok groceries. Geoff works from about 8.45 in the morning till 12.30 and from 2.30 till 4.30.

He has had a very hectic first week being introduced to numerous people. Some of these have been Thais and meeting them has involved social occasions like lunch parties or dinner parties or just meeting for a drink. I have been invited to some of these in order to offset the Thai wives, and incredible though it may seem Geoff and I both feel that we don't want to go to another night club for a very long time. We have twice watched the same Filippino girl sing songs to the accompaniment of her Filippino guitar at Bangkok's newest and poshest hotel. We have seen three French girls do a five minute roller-skating turn which is supposed to take your breath away. We have seen three bored-looking Thai girls singing American songs for a large crowd of young Thai people to dance to. We have had the opportunity to dance to five different dance orchestras. We have eaten Japanese and Chinese food (both with chop-sticks). We have had lunch with a Thai ex-ambassador to London and dinner with General Phao, Minister of the Interior and head of police, a highly significant figure in Thai politics. And quite apart from these activities we've been to a cocktail party given by the counsellor and met a great many British diplomats and other bods and their wives and attended a reception at the Portuguese Embassy given in honour of the Portuguese national day, and there we met diplomats of a great many different nationalities.

All this, as you can imagine, is a far step from life in St.

Albans. The main difficulty is making conversation, especially with people who don't speak English very well. From the feminine point of view clothes aren't a great problem as nobody wears hats or stockings or gloves ever, so you only have to worry about not wearing the same dress too many times in quick succession.

We went to church at the English church on our first Sunday here. The padre was an Episcopalian Scot with a very refined Glasgow accent and the service he conducted was a pretty high one, though all denominations are invited to attend. There weren't a great many people there, certainly no diplomats, and we asked him if this was normal when we met him at the counsellor's cocktail party. He laughed and said that diplomats had other things to do on Sundays. We said that we would always go to church, but sure enough last Sunday Geoff had to take somebody out to the airport in the car during church hours last Sunday, and this coming week-end he's taking the diplomatic bag down to some town in the very south of Thailand and I'm going with him. We either fly or go by train and we stay the night with the consul there. So much for church!

When Geoff came back from the airport on Sunday we were driven to the sea-side by a friend. It took about 1½ hours to get to the beach and we drove through flat paddy-fields and villages where the houses were made of wood and built on stocks (because of rising floods during the rainy season) and the small children run about naked. We also saw about three hills which looked rather odd sticking up out of the plain. They were covered with trees and looked green and attractive if you didn't think about the snakes and things that lived there. The beach was a highly civilised affair, built up with bungalows large and small belonging to the richer inhabitants of Bangkok, and, nearer the sea, little huts which you could take and swim from. We had a rice and ham and egg lunch at a café first and then we took a hut and swam. The water was very warm but fairly rough so we enjoyed a good buffetting and afterwards got a little tanned by the sea-breeze. The sun was mostly hidden behind clouds so the heat was bearable. It made a very pleasant change from Bangkok and I believe that British people, especially those with children, spend several days on end there during the pleasant weather round about Christmas. During August and September when our children will be here it won't be so easy to get there because the rains will have made the roads difficult.

Wat Benchamabophit in Bangkok

For my sight-seeing I went to see four Buddhist temples, or Wats, as they're called. These are very colourful and quite extraordinary places with lots of curiously shaped roofs and pinnacles about them. Really, I find it quite impossible to describe them but I've taken photographs and will try and gather more concrete ideas about them as time goes by and report again. The main feature is the image of Buddha who takes the place of the altar in Christian Religions. Usually he is large and golden-looking (only one is made of pure gold) and sitting cross-legged with one hand raised or both hands at rest. But in one temple (called the Temple of the Reclining Buddha) he is forty feet long and lying down. These temples all had monasteries attached to them and there were a great many young monks about. These always wear a sort of toga the colour of our yellow dusters at home so they are easily distinguishable. It's normal for all young men to do a three months' novitiate in a monastery so a lot of the monks look very young indeed.

Monks and Buddha in Phutthamonthon

[Handwritten note to Margaret]

Mummy told me about her "click" when she last wrote. This doesn't convey anything to me but I hope she's going to be all right.

Love to all the family - Averin

Menu for a Chinese Meal

given for General Phao
at a private room at the OASIS

Hors d'Oeuvre
Sharks Fins
Roast Sucking Pi
(skin only eaten, electric light bulbs in eye sockets)
Devilled chicken legs and wings
Pigeons' eggs
Manchurian Duck
Sweet-sour fish
Fried rice
Alaska ice cream
(ice-cream inside warm meringue casing)
Fruit and coffee

Each course was put in a large dish or bowl in the middle of a table and everybody helped themselves with chopsticks, putting the food into little bowls provided for the purpose. For sloppy courses with lots of gravy the 'boy' dished it out with a spoon and the eaters were provided with little china spoons. The bowls were changed between courses and sometimes the boys brought round steaming hot towels dipped in eau de Cologne for us to wipe our hands on. The men wiped their faces too, though this wasn't strictly necessary as the room was air-conditioned.

Each diner was given a small bowl containing soya sauce, and the idea was to dip the tips of your chop-sticks into this before taking up a morsel and putting it in the mouth. Other sauces were provided for other courses. We were given whisky and soda to drink but the Thais had hot China tea which must be frequently topped up or replaced, and when we tried this we found it most refreshing as an antidote to the oily gravies.

The party was somewhat lopsided as two of the guests' wives were at home with flu and one present wife obviously felt ill. (It was during the flu epidemic.)

General Phao didn't bother to speak much English. Colonel Thana, his youthful and valiant right-hand man had to interpret for him.

Cost of the dinner for 8 people: 1800 ticals, i.e. about £31.

General Phao

NOTES

General Phao was Minister of the Interior and director general of Thailand's national police until September 1957, when he was ousted in one of the many coups d'état that took place in Thailand in the 1950s. According to Wikipedia he was "notorious for his excesses against political opponents".

11th June (2): "Strange animals"

46 Lang Suan Lane,
Bangkok.

June 11th, 1957

My darling Ann and Michael,

I'm going to write to you two separately because I feel you may be bored with some of the things I say to the grown-ups.

Our poor dog - I know now that his name is Doddick - is ill and has had to go to the vet who says he has distemper. This is a kind of doggy flu. Why did he have to wait until we came to be ill, I wonder? I haven't the faintest idea how to look after dogs. But fortunately Sam See and her mother love him dearly and are quite willing to look after him tenderly.

We also have a cat but he doesn't come into the house much. Beg your pardon: she. She had some kittens yesterday but nobody knows how many there are because she climbed up between a roof and a balcony to have them and we can only hear their squeaking.

There are plenty of other strange animals around (quite apart from the mosquitoes who nibble us to bits; I'm sure they'll introduce themselves to you hungrily when you come out here). For instance there are a lot of frogs who hop around on the verandah at night-time. When it rains in the evening after dark they are so very happy that they croak so loud we can hardly hear ourselves talk. And then again the bull-frog makes quite a different noise. He sounds like a cow mooing. When it rains at night a great many animals chirrup and squeak and twitter and honk and I imagine it's rather like being in the jungle, only not quite so noisy.

Every evening when the lights are out a lot of little lizards, about three inches long, come out of the ceiling and eat mosquitoes and moths and flies. And then there's another lizard, much larger, called a Tock-A, who is rather a formidable fellow. He is said to have teeth and to bite you if you're so foolish as to be unkind to him. Fortunately he lives outside under the eaves and only strays into the house by mistake. He makes a noise rather like a cuckoo with a bass voice. He says, "Tock-A, Tock-A, Tock-A" and if he does this seven times it's supposed to be very lucky.

I'm sending you each a picture postcard of a Buddhist temple or Wat, because I went to see four Wats yesterday. The roof of yours, Ann, is painted gold and really looks rather smashing, and in yours, Michael, there are all sorts of greens and blues and reds and golds.

Wat Saket (Golden Mount)

Most people in Thailand are Buddhists, which means that they aren't Christians. Buddha lived more than 2,000 years ago and he preached to the people, telling them to love each other and behave themselves rather like Jesus did. And in the end he ascended into heaven too. One difference between the Buddhist religion and ours is that we believe in life after death but they believe that when they die their souls are born again in another body on earth. If they're very good in this life they may be born again as somebody rather better off and have an easier life. On the other hand, if they're very naughty they may be born again as an animal. For this reason they don't really like killing animals in case they're killing one of their ancestors.

Thank you, Michael, for your letter of June 2nd. Cricket seems to be doing well, and we do glean information about the rest of your life from Granpa! Have you done any composing recently? If you have, or if there's anything else you'd like Daddy and me to have a look at you can always send it by bag. It would take about five weeks to get here but we'd get it back to you eventually. The same applies to you, Ann. Shove on any drawings or tests or what have you so we can admire your handiwork.

With lots of love from Mummy

13th June: "Almost every thinkable nationality"

QUEEN'S BIRTHDAY

June 13th 1957

All wives who aren't working asked to arrive at the Residency at 9.30 a.m. equipped with flowers and vases (especially tall and large round ones) and ash-trays and cigarette boxes. On the appointed day the lawn in front of the residency is already bedecked with shields and there are three Union Jacks flying.

Getting ready for the Queen's birthday at the Residency

Inside the residency is all a-bustle. Servants, both male and female, hover round to give help. Head of Chancery's wife is in charge and as soon as we arrive we are given two enormous bronze bowls and told to fill them. In order to help support the flowers each contains an empty tin that once held Nestlés powdered milk and an empty jam jar. Our small offering is not nearly sufficient to fill one of these bowls but fortunately, outside the pantry, there is a large table strewn with flowers and everybody is helping themselves liberally to these.

We admire each others' work and offer advice. When vases are filled we carry them through and are proud to see them placed in the drawing-room, the dining-room or hall, or in one of the spacious corridors.

Outside in the garden men are at work fitting coloured lights and setting up a marquee for the band. The word QUEEN, fitted with coloured bulbs, lies disconsolate on the ground and we wonder in what context it is going to appear.

Inside the main entrance, an enormous crown on the floor, and behind that a table with a silver-framed photograph of the queen and a silver bowl of roses.

At last the ladies' work is complete and servants are gathering up the débris. Exhausted, for it is very hot, we stroll over to the head-of-chancery's house and there refresh ourselves with iced grapefruit juice.

Everybody hopes that it will not rain but in this tropical country the rainy season has already begun and after lunch, sure enough, we have the heaviest downfall yet experienced this year. By four o'clock there are enormous pools on the Embassy lawn and everybody is trying to accustom himself to the idea that when the party begins at 6 there will be 1500 people inside the Residency whose rooms are spacious but not as spacious as all that. There are ceiling fans, but among so many people, what is a ceiling fan?

The Embassy staff gather, as ordered, at 5.30. We step gingerly onto the garden path (for it has stopped raining) and although no directive is given it is generally assumed that the party will, after all, be out of doors. The pools have miraculously disappeared and although the ladies' heels sink into the lawn this muddy fact is ignored. In this humid climate it is stickily hot and men's faces are bathed in perspiration, while ladies' dresses (cocktail cottons for easy washing) are already moistly creased in spite of the fact that they have recently received the attentions of the washing amah's iron. The men are wearing white, or light, tropical suits and these are looking somewhat rumpled too.

The word QUEEN is still lying on the ground but on the far side of the artificial lake the words GOD and THE have been put in place and by 6 o'clock SAVE and QUEEN have been miraculously inserted and the whole intercession is illuminated.

Just before 6 o'clock the first guests arrive. The chargé d'affaires receives them at the head of the Residency stairs, where they are promptly retrieved and passed onwards by specially appointed gentlemen of the Embassy. Through the hall they go, past those now slightly drooping flowers, and down the steps into the garden and here more appointed gentlemen encourage them to spread themselves about the lawns.

As darkness falls all is lit up by clusters of coloured lights which hang charmingly from the trees, and a mercifully cooling breeze stirs. This has been an open invitation to all who would care to come and by now the lawn is filled with diplomats and politicians and businessmen of almost every thinkable nationality. To the hosts and hostesses the language problem is frequently great but conversation is somehow maintained.

Guests at the Queen's birthday party

Somewhere to the right a pipe band strikes up and the whole company drifts over to an enclosure to watch the marching antics of two bands supplied by the local police and military authorities. When this is over there is another drift back to the centre of the lawn. Servants are dodging speedily among the crowds to make sure that everybody's glass is filled, and presently we hear the voice of the chargé d'affaires over the loud-speaker and he is proposing a toast to the Queen of Great Britain and the Commonwealth of Nations. The band (this time a naval one) plays the British National anthem at a sprightly pace. We raise our glasses and murmur, "The Queen". Next, with their national anthem, comes the toast to the Sovereign of the peoples on whose soil we stand, and then, before conversation becomes general again we are invited to raise our eyes to the first floor of the Residency where a screen has been stretched across the balcony and a colour film of the Trooping of the Colours is ingeniously projected from within. It all seems very far away and we feel that an issue of opera glasses all round would help, but for those who are finding conversation difficult it at least provides a distraction.

Now, apart from occasional accompaniment from the band, official entertainment is over and there is nothing but conversation left. The party is scheduled to end at 8 o'clock. At 8.15 the chargé d'affaires leaves. At 8.30 the bar closes and the band departs, but there is still a hard core of some 200 guests left. Finally, when it is nearly 9 o'clock, the British diplomats and their wives, exhausted from 3½ hours of standing, droop wearily away, leaving behind them those happy guests who are too content to tear themselves away ...

Conversations:

Hardened French diplomat: *Bangkok is a dreary place. Thais who have been to England admit this themselves. There is no cultural life, no food for the spirit.*

Hardened British businessman: *You'll have a wonderful time here. Everybody loves Bangkok.*

N.B. *No hats, no gloves, no stockings.*

16th June: " I thought he had been hit by a bullet"

TRAIN JOURNEY TO SONGKHLA
(to take diplomatic bag to Consulate)

June 16th 1957

It was very hot when we arrived at the station at two o'clock in the afternoon. The car was immediately besieged by scruffy-looking men and boys who wanted to carry our luggage but we waved them away and left Wirut in charge of the car while we went to find out about the train. It was easy enough to find the platform which was crowded with Thais. There was an engine there, attached to a few coaches, and we had just handed one small bag to the attendant (he tried to take the diplomatic bag but G. snatched this back and I gave him the small bag to show there was no ill-feeling) when the train drew out of the station and disappeared up the line.

Express train at Bangkok station 1950s

G. went back to see about the luggage, which included several crates of beer and one of Pimm's no.1 (a present from the departed ambassador) for the Consul at Songkhla. He took ages over this, because the luggage had to be weighed, and there was I on the platform, getting more and more worried, with the time of departure drawing near, and no Geoff, and no train and me with no knowledge of Thai and almost no money. However, G. and the luggage appeared at last and the train reappeared, and we got into the last coach which belonged to Malayan Railways and was presumably going through to Penang and seemed rather comfortable. But we were in the wrong compartment and had to turn out and went into another coach which was not nearly so comfortable. We had a First Class sleeper compartment, consisting of one rather narrow plastic-covered seat facing a wooden partition. A creaking, turning fan tried to cool us from above. There was a wash-basin in one corner of the compartment and a small table which could be put up beneath the window. There was a glass window which could be put up and also a shutter covered with a fine mosquito mesh.

The train started half-an-hour late. We were both exhausted with the heat and could only sit and stare dazedly at the outskirts of Bangkok as they went slowly by, and presently the banana and mango and coconut groves and after that the grey, dry paddy-fields. Presently we summoned enough energy to stagger along to the dining-car where we ordered tea, an iced drink in glasses, so diluted as to be almost tasteless, and costing 1 tical (about 4d) for the two of us.

The train stopped at quite a number of stations but in between times it gathered speed. It was drawn by twin diesel engines and sounded its horn (yes, it was more like a horn or a ship's hooter than a train's whistle) to warn people off the line or to tell us when it was about to leave a station. We passed numerous herds of cows which looked just like Jersey cattle, and flocks of goats and sheep which were tended by boys or men or women, the men in loose navy blue cotton shirts and shorts and the women in blouses and sarongs, and all wearing conical or flat-topped or broad-brimmed straw hats. Nearer to Songkhla cows seemed to give way to buffalo.

Villages by the wayside all consisted of wooden huts on stilts, mostly with roofs made of coconut palms; indeed some of the huts were made of these. We caught glimpses of people fast asleep inside their huts and children, mostly naked - especially the boys - playing about outside. In Rajburi we saw a group of three children, two boys and a girl, playing about by a well, watched indifferently by their mother. All the children were naked and the bigger boy hid modestly from us behind a wall for a time but then he wanted to join in the others' game and abandoned modesty for the sake of enjoyment.

Water seemed to play a great part in the villagers' lives. Every khlong and river had people swimming in it, or women washing themselves or their clothes or men wading about with water up to their necks, not bathing, I think, but manipulating invisible fishing nets. There were few people working in the paddyfields but in the evening we passed farms where the whole family seemed to be busy doing something, hoeing with a crude implement, or looking after the animals or tending the paddy-field.

By 6.30 the whole countryside was bathed in the wonderful light of the late afternoon. An astonishing crop of hills had suddenly sprung up out of the plain, like giants' teeth, and at 7 o'clock, when to the left and East of us everything was already in darkness, these were still lit with a faint western glow, and in the sky above them one star shone faintly.

After that there was very little to see. In the East the night is really black and we only caught sight of an occasional glow from some hut's single lamp or fire, and could just discern the shape of trees beside the track. Small towns presented a great splash of light and activity and noise, and then all was dark again.

We went along to the dining-car for dinner. There were only four other diners there, two Chinese and an American and a Thai, but perhaps this was because a European dinner was served - soup, fish, meat, and caramel pudding, followed by coffee which was so strong that it was almost thick. The custom among Thais seemed to be to have their meals brought to them in their compartments and one waiter who looked worn out long before the evening was over was rushing about with bowls of rice covered with sauces and meat and eggs. He also served drinks to all the travellers - local beer, 7-Up (fizzy lemonade), Green Spot and the ever-popular coke.

The chief dining-car attendant (who spent his whole time at a table making out bills) could speak English and took us under his wing, getting up to come and take our orders himself. Perhaps he was impressed by the diplomatic bag which Geoffrey was still clutching. We didn't realise how fortunate we were in this until we were on the return journey to Bangkok, when nobody could understand a word we said. But more of that anon. A solemn, round-eyed young man clad in white shirt and long dark blue trousers laid the table for us with great care and precision, piece by piece, and we contrasted him mentally with the English dining-car waiter who throws the cutlery onto the table with a great clatter.

When we returned to our compartment it was only 8 o'clock but the bunks were already made up, with a single bottom sheet, pillow and one folded blanket. What had been the back of the one seat had now been swung up to form the second bunk, making everything much more roomy; in fact, the whole thing looked so restful that we very soon went to bed and one of us, at least, slept very well until 7 o'clock next morning.

In the centre of the coach there was a bathroom complete with shower and water stored in a huge jar and a scoop to scoop the water out with but somehow we didn't quite like to use this. The Thais, men and women, were wandering about in sarongs, the women with blouses on top, and we felt rather conspicuous with our European dressing-gowns. The Thais continued in their disattire until well into the morning, which seemed a good way of preventing their day clothes from getting creased in the damp heat.

Breakfast in the dining-car consisted of a banana each, more thick black coffee, toast, butter which someone seemed to have forgotten to put in the refrigerator the night before & had turned rancid, and a choice of jam or marmalade - or what was left of both these confitures in the bottom of two rather dirty jam-jars.

At one o'clock we arrived at Haad Yai and here we left the train, jumping down onto the sanded track, while our faithful berth attendant handed our cases and all the packing cases out through the window. We stood for perhaps five minutes in the gruelling sunshine with a crowd of interested samlor-drivers and would-be porters round us, and then at last Geoffrey went up on to the station platform and found the consul looking for us and soon our luggage was stowed in the boot and the back of his car and he was driving us at terrifying speed, consular flag flying, the last 20 kilometres or so to Songkhla.

Songkhla is a small port and fishing town with busy streets and thousands of samlors and bicycles - the latter ridden by men, women and children alike. These bicycles are made in Thailand and the fashion seems to be to have the saddle far too high for the length of leg which must make them very uncomfortable for the rider. The Consulate is a large, square white building, perhaps 500 yards from the sea, with a great stretch of green from the house towards the beach, and the Union Jack fluttering from the flag-pole from dawn to dusk. Upstairs there was a suite of two bedrooms in the centre and giving onto a wide corridor or balcony on three sides. Our bedroom had 6 half swing-doors, with about two feet of space below and unlimited space above, opening onto the corridors and balcony, and we found this rather disconcerting owing to the feeling that at any moment some mischievous person might disturb our privacy by peering under a door. Needless to say this didn't happen, and the servants were so discreet that when next day I wanted to get hold of one of them to have a dress ironed they both rushed away from their cleaning operations at the first sound of my approaching footsteps. I never did succeed in tracking them down and in the end, Susan, the consul's 16-year-old daughter and lady of the house, advised me to put the dress on the back of a dining-room chair from where it miraculously disappeared and reappeared in my bedroom, ironed, some hours later.

It must have been quite a quarter to two when we arrived at the Consulate, hot and sticky, and we were a little agitated to find the makings of an informal luncheon party - the only other British member of the Consulate staff and his wife and two American members of USIS - waiting for us. We had showers and changed as quickly as we could, but when we came downstairs the party had broken into the case of Pims No.1 and wasn't in the least interested in eating. One bottle of Pims finished, the consul started on a second, and it wasn't until we were well into the middle of this that Susan read out the instructions and pointed out that one bottle should be enough to make up 7 pints of the drink. I don't know about anybody else, but I floated very dizzily into the dining-room when lunch was at last served at 3 o'clock, and my condition was only slightly relieved by the excellent curry which we were given. After lunch Geoffrey and I both felt inclined to sleep but we were swept into the garden whereother Americans were waiting for a game of tennis with the consul. Not having suitable clothes for this we played a more gentle game of badminton with Susan and Mrs. Clark and two Thai lads who turned up, a youth of 18 who was eager to practise his English, and a small boy of perhaps 12 who spoke not a word but wielded a very skilful left-handed racquet.

I had been told that there was excellent swimming to be had in Songkhla and had brought my swim-suit with me, and I bullied so much that on the morning before we left (we only spent two nights there) it was arranged that Susan and I should go down to the beach. We changed into our swimsuits at the consulate, wrapped towels round our shoulders and were driven over the rough scrub in a land-rover by the consulate driver. Geoffrey had no more work to do so he came with us, equipped with a hat which was far too small for his big head to protect him from the sun. The driver promised to come back for us in half-an-hour, so we skipped gleefully over the oven-hot sand and plunged into the sea which was clear and calm and blue. When we were about knee-deep Susan spotted a jelly-fish, and then she saw another, and finally there were so many that we knew we couldn't possibly swim. So there we were for half-an-hour, occasionally dipping under the water and quickly nipping up again, expecting to be stung at any moment, and Geoffrey pacing up and down the beach, tiny hat on large head, and here and there along the water's edge, Thai fish-spotters perched on forked poles and seemingly oblivious of our dilemma.

As the driver took us home he told us he had forgotten to mention that there were sharks at that particular place ....

After two nights in Songkhla we returned to Bangkok. This time the Clarks drove us to Haad Yai, in the Consul's car but at a slightly more sedate pace. The train was already waiting for us and when Geoffrey had bought our tickets (there were three for each of us) we got into our reserved compartment, which at first seemed more modern and better equipped than the one on our journey down, but this turned out to be a sad illusion as far as the rest of the train was concerned. The train down to Songkhla had been going on to Penang, in Malaya, but this was an all-Thai train and had come from Kota Bahru in the South-East of Thailand, and for some reason the whole standard of service and cleanliness was very much lower.

On one side of our compartment there were two monks and on the other a bathroom, and beyond that two monks, in their yellow wrap-rounds and accompanied by the inevitable string-bag and umbrella. Somebody (perhaps a monk) was taking a basketful of durian, a fruit which is said to taste delicious but smells like nothing on earth, with them and had conceived the bright idea of putting the basket in the bathroom. From there it gave out powerful odours which permeated our compartment and ruined the whole journey for me. There are some smells which you can come accustomed to and in the end forget about, but this was one which seemed to worsen with time.

Soon after we had started we felt thirsty and Geoffrey managed to engage the attention of the waiter who was rushing busily along the corridor. He was trying to express the idea of beer in signs when there was a sudden metallic clatter and Geoffrey, clutching the back of his neck, began to sink in a stunned fashion towards the floor. I managed to seize him and, with the help of the attendant, dragged him onto the seat, and presently he found courage to take his hand away from his neck and was obviously surprised - as we all were - to find that it wasn't covered in blood. I thought he had been hit by a bullet and am sure he thought the same. Not that there was any reason to suppose that he might be shot at, but somehow in a foreign country one imagines that bullets fly more freely than in one's own.

The mystery was solved by the attendant who spotted a large, rough stone on the floor and we realised that some small boy must have thrown it in in the way that small boys do. The monks on either side of us were most concerned and immediately produced a bottle of what was obviously Sloane's liniment. The inscriptions were in Thai and Chinese, but there was a large portrait of Mr. Sloane himself, complete with enormous bushy mustache, and Geoffrey insisted that I should put some of it on his neck (which now had a small egg on it) although it increased the pain by a formidable burning sensation.

Meanwhile, with recollections of first aid knowledge gleaned at home, I wanted to apply a cold compress, but as no water in Thailand is ever cold I couldn't quite see how to manage this until I remembered the ice that is served in drinks. I asked the waiter for ice in a glass but of course he didn't understand and after failing miserably to describe ice in sign language I wrote ICE IN A GLASS on a piece of paper and gave it to him. He disappeared and came back presently, not only with ice in a glass, but with the beer which Geoffrey had originally ordered, so while I applied ice in a handkerchief to the back of his neck he refreshed himself with a long cool drink. He was quite grateful for the ice as he said it cancelled out the burning pain from Sloane's Liniment.

25th June:
"Getting to know Bangkok"

British Embassy,
Bangkok

June 25th, 1957

Dear Everybody,

I suppose we're getting to know Bangkok fairly well by now, with having to find our way to various places. It's a great, sprawling place, completely unplanned, with roads roaming about in all directions. There are also canals here and there, which is why it is called the Venice of the East. I haven't been to Venice but I really can't imagine there's much similarity between the two places. I can't imagine the Venice canals are as muddy and slimy and smelly as these. However, junks do move about upon some of them and then of course the river is a very busy place indeed with lots of water traffic bustling about.

The most common means of propulsion everywhere is the samlor, a sort of tricycle with a shaded seat between the back wheels. The seat holds two people at a pinch and the samlor is ridden by a man who wears navy blue cotton shirt and shorts and a straw hat and some sort of sandal or delapidated shoe or nothing at all on his feet. He has the right of way in all traffic and avails himself of this privilege to the irritating full. He sails along in the middle of the road and shoots off to the right or left without any warning. (Incidentally driving is on the left side of the road.) He's a sort of cheap form of taxi-driver and Europeans use him as well as the locals. There are other taxis as well, usually small Austin vans, and they're a highly dangerous means of transport because they whizz about at a terrifying speed. The reason for this, I'm told, is that the taxi-driver (unlike the samlor-driver, who owns his own vehicle) hires his car by the day and must fit in as many journeys as possible to make any sort of profit! There are also bumbling, top-heavy buses which try to blast all other traffic off the road with their horns which sound rather like the hooter of an American express train, and trams, which are a great nuisance because the roads are so narrow. So if you want to go anywhere you've got plenty of transportation to choose from, but personally I prefer to ring up the office and ask Geoff if the car and driver are available!

One day this week we were invited to lunch with General Phao who (as I've said before) is Minister of something-or-Other and Head of Police. The reason why we have to do with him is that Geoff's job involves a certain amount of liaison with the Thai Police. He is said to be a very corrupt gentleman. For instance, with one hand he is "trying" to stamp out the drug traffic, while with the other he is putting a large proportion of the profits from the drug traffic in his own pocket. However, corruption plays a large part in all Thai life and politics so one mustn't judge him too harshly!

Thai gentlemen also have a very irresponsible attitude towards marriage. The normal thing, I believe, is to have a wife and some children and one or two mistresses as well. Some even have a number two wife, but this is rather an expensive proposition because of keeping up several establishments. General Phao has a very charming and amusing wife who lives in a house by herself, and their adopted daughter, a charming girl of 17, has her own house and ménage too. I think the lunch was in Madame Phao's house, but I'm not quite sure. There were eight of us altogether, 4 British and 4 Thais and first of all we sat in a smallish room (air-conditioned) on wooden chairs studded with mother-of-pearl, round a ditto table, and had drinks passed to us and nibbles made by Madame Phao herself. Then we moved to the dining-room (also air-conditioned) and sat on more wooden chairs studded with mother-of-pearl round a ditto table. There were in the same room a cupboard and a sort of divan-thing and a chest made of the same materials and Madame Phao told us that they had been given her by her mother as a wedding present and imported from China.

The lunch was a farewell lunch to the departing air-attaché and his wife (British) and when we had finished eating General Phao presented the air attaché with a silver cigarette box and ash tray while Madame Phao gave his wife a length of Thai silk. We had hors d'heuvres (with caviarre) and a meat course followed by a Thai curry and a rather stodgy sweet made of tapioca covered with coconut blancmange. Fortunately it seemed quite polite to leave portions of every course on one's plate and everybody left large portions of the tapioca to show how well satisfied they were. Finally we had coffee and then after a suitable length of conversation (General Phao doesn't speak much English so most of the conversation was interpreted by Colonel Tana, his right-hand man) we rose and departed.

We had another meal – dinner this time – with some Chinese friends of ours called Wong one day. To say they are Chinese is rather misleading because in fact they are now naturalised English and call themselves Henry and Sophie, though these are not their real names, of course. Henry works in the British Information Service which copes with propaganda of the British way of life to the Thais. They have a grown-up son who is in England (at London University, I think) and an adopted daughter who has just got married. This dinner was also to say farewell to the departing air-attaché and it was a very special dinner cooked by Chinese cooks specially imported for the purpose. We had it sitting out on the veranda and there were the usual number of courses associated with Chinese meals – about 10, I think. Henry and Sophie sat side by side at the round table and doled out food from the central dish. We ate from Chinese bowls with ivory chopsticks, though for gravies and so forth china spoons were provided. We started off with sharks fins in gravy and then waded through all sorts of other delicacies like goose's feet and pigeons' wings and legs and pigeons' eggs and fried prawns, ending up with a dish of birds nest with some sort of fruit. The birds nest was white and rather gluey

(I expect you know the nest is made with the spittle of the bird and all the other things like straw and twigs are extracted before it's cooked). We asked Henry why the Chinese lay such store by the goose's feet and sharks fins etc. and he said that these are the strong parts of the animal's body and were originally supposed to impart strength to the body of the human who ate them. I think Sophie still believes that they do.

I talked to Henry about Lin Yu Tang (pronounced Tong) and was interested to hear he knew him quite well because they were in the same year together, presumably at the University. They don't see much of each other, especially as Lin Yu Tang is in America.

I have already embarked on my teaching career but I'll tell you about that next week.

Geoff had a day in bed on Friday. Nothing special wrong. He just felt limp. This is quite a common occurrence among Europeans and he is trying to remember to take more salt tablets to counteract further indispositions.

Much love, Averin

[Handwritten note to Margaret]

I wonder if I could ask you to do something for me, and that is to find out if it's possible to have supplies of Volpar Paste sent out by bag?! I meant to ask our chemist about it but left it too late & he was out when I called on the last day. The only address they give on the tube is the British Drug Houses Ltd., London, which seems vague in the extreme.

I went to the so-called "British Dispensary" in Bangkok the other day and asked for V.P. The girl didn't understand so she asked a man, & presently there were six of them all concentrating on me with great interest. At last one man said, "What is this thing?" and I said coldly,* "a contraceptive." "Oh, you mean a birth control jelly?" he said. "We only have an American one called Ramses." I bought this "vaginal jelly" (the only way it *describes itself: discretion seems to forbid further enlightenment, and how am I to know it will actually control birth?) for the horrid sum of about 9/-.*

*Coldly is the wrong word. I fairly sweated with embarrassment.

    So you see I'm in a dilemma and have uncomfortable visions of lots more little Hintons over-running the place. If you could arrange for some chemist, or Messrs. Drug Houses Ltd. to send a regular supply of, say, 4 every 6 weeks c/o the Foreign Office, Whitehall, London, S.W.1, Please forward by bag to Bangkok (U.K. Postage), I should be deeply grateful. Geoff too, for that matter. And if you'll let me know by air-letter how much money is involved I'll send you a cheque right away.

NOTES

Lin Yu Tang was a prolific writer of books in both Chinese and English. Many of his works aimed to bridge the cultural gap between East and West. He was nominated for the Nobel Prize in Literature in 1940 and 1950.

25th June (2): "Daddy walking about in his socks"

British Embassy,
Bangkok

June 25th, 1957

My darling Ann and Michael,

Good news of you from Granny this week, Ann, and thank you, Michael, for your letter of the 16th. I also had another letter from Mrs. Lowes telling us about Ann's last days with them. She seemed a little hurt because Gillian told her that Ann had told Gillian she was an old fusspot because she wouldn't let her swim with Fuzz. Daddy and I had a big giggle about this but, darling Ann, you'll have to be careful not to say these things that may be passed on! I hope you thanked her <u>very</u> much for having you to stay. She seems to have tried hard to make you happy.

Doddick the dog is now nearly better after his distemper, you'll be glad to hear. He's got to go to the vet to have one more injection, but he doesn't seem to mind these at all. He goes in great state in the car, driven by Wirut the driver and with either cookie or Sam See or her mother to hold his hand. In fact he enjoys the trips so much that whenever the car is at the door and the door opens he tries to climb in and has to be hauled out again. He's supposed to spend the night outside the house (it's not cold, remember) but one night he refused to budge, so I let him stay. In the early morning I thought I heard him whining so I crept downstairs and found him fast asleep in a chair, the naughty old thing! No more indoor sleeping for Master Doddick!

Sam See and her mother are very nice. Sam See is a clever little girl (although she's 14 I don't think she's taller than you, Ann) and she knows quite a lot of English words. She and her mother never wear shoes in the house, in fact I think most Thais take off their shoes at the door and walk about in bare feet. When I ask to see Cookie he comes over from his kitchen in shoes which are just a wooden sole with a band across, kicks them off by the steps and pops in in bare feet. English ladies often do the same. If you go to dinner with friends you say, "Do you mind if I take my shoes off?" and the friends say, "Of course not," so you take them off and feel very comfortable. Some English men do it too, and, of course, children! I have even seen Daddy walking about in his socks! Thai women never wear stockings, even on the most important occasions, and the children never wear socks.

We went to dinner with some Chinese friends called Mr. and Mrs. Wong the other day. They gave us real Chinese food which we ate with ivory chopsticks out of small china bowls. There were about ten courses, starting off with sharks' fins in gravy and then pigeons' legs and wings and goose's feet and pigeons' eggs and rice and various kinds of fish and ending up with special birds nest which the birds stick together with their spittle and which is considered a very great delicacy! It's quite difficult eating with chop-sticks at first. You have to hold them both in the same hand and some slippery foods are apt to slip on to the table-cloth before you can get them into your mouth! However, nobody minds, and you don't go away feeling hungry. In fact, with so many courses you go away feeling so full that you can hardly get up from the table!

Lots of love, Mummy

2nd July: "I have ... built up quite a clientèle"

British Embassy,
Bangkok

July 2nd, 1957

Dear Everybody,

I think I'd better start this week by giving you news of all the children because although they write to us often and regularly they don't have time to write to all the grown-ups.

Ann, Michael and Jill in St Albans, 1957

Ann has been very busy taking all sorts of different exams. She took a music theory exam (was it Grade II or Grade III, Ann?) on June 19th and on the 22nd she took her second ballet exam in London. She and others went up with their ballet teacher in a coach and they had a sandwich lunch on the way. Then from June 24th - 28th she was having school exams and on the 11th July she's going to take her Grade II piano exam. She's also passed her swimming test at school and is now learning to dive. Sorry I spelt towkay wrong, Ann, but I've never seen it written down and tried to spell it the way it sounds.

Michael's main occupation seems to be cricket. He plays in innumerable games of which I quite lose count and takes a fair number of wickets but doesn't make many runs. He swims once a week at the Cowley baths and is now a 'frog' which means he can swim a width. During the early part of the heat-wave they were taken for an extra swim on a Sunday and Michael came home in the headmaster's car and was given an ice lolly "which tasted very nice". I hate to think of him wearing his thick flannel shirts and trousers in the weather you've been having and hope (but not too hopefully) that they've been allowed to shed some clothes. Granpa says he looks very well and we also gather from him that Michael does appear in chapel at the right times and sings lustily there.

Jill has both her two top front teeth out. She goes down to the beach very often and enjoys the water, but I don't think she's swimming yet. She goes to brownies once a week and when it's fine she takes her tea with her and they have the meeting on the beach. This is the Par village pack and I think Jill is the only girl boarder who goes. There are only two other girl boarders who are sisters; the other 11 are boys. They have had their sports day and Mr. Tomlinson tries to teach her cricket with the rest of her form. The only report so far is that she doesn't seem to have the makings of a good batsman! Mrs. Tomlinson is pleased with her school work and my letters are being used as a basis for her form's geography lessons! They followed our journey on a map and now I have to do my best to keep up their interest in Bangkok.

And now for some of our own news. I have got well on with my teaching of English and have built up quite a clientèle. The prime minister's nephew, a lad of nineteen or twenty, comes to me for three hours a week and a man who is trying to get a scholarship to Colombo university comes for six hours a week, two hours at a time. Twice a week I go to lecture at the Chulalongkorn University, once to the 1st year Pharmacy students and once to the 2nd year Pharmacy students. The whole university seems to be gathered together in one huge compound and between lectures the place is swarming with young men and women, the girls all wearing white blouses and black or navy blue skirts and the men white shirts and dark trousers. As they all have dark hair too the effect is quite striking. They are so short of space that the 1st year Pharmacy class is in an outdoor shelter with a curved roof made, I think, of plaited coconut palms (dried). This doesn't come right down to the ground which is concreted except for an aisle up the middle, and this becomes very muddy and puddly after rain. There are 160 students in the class and I have to speak into a hand-microphone, so I hold the mike in one hand and a book in the other, and then when I have to write something on the blackboard I have quite a juggle-around trying to decide whether to do without the mike or the book.

My only other class consists of about 15 Social Workers who want to learn English because their text-books are all in English, and I take them twice a week at the Ministry of Culture. For this much work I can earn about £10 a week and we're trying hard to save most of it for harder times ahead when we get posted back to England. There's a small matter of a house to buy and three children to send to good schools ......

Averin teaching English

One day this week Daddy had to get out of bed at 4.30 a.m. to go to the Embassy to unlock the safe to give the diplomatic bags to the courier who had to take them to Vien-tiane, the capital of Laos, by plane. He had to set the alarm for 4 o'clock, and prrrrrrr, we both woke up, and he got dressed rather grumpily, and then I went back to sleep while he went downstairs and waited on the verandah, where Doddick came to greet him and started wuffing in a quiet but business-like kind of way in case there were any burglars about. Presently an Embassy car came for Daddy and he went and unlocked the safe and locked it up again and by 5 o'clock he was back in bed. We had told the servants all this was going to happen (in case they thought there were burglars about) but they thought Daddy was going away somewhere by plane and were most astonished when he came down to breakfast with me.

I wonder what sort of a picture you have in your minds of Bangkok, if you have any picture at all? If you think of the main shopping centre as something like Oxford Street in London, or St. Peter's Street in St. Albans or the High in Oxford you'll have to think again because it isn't like any of these. All the shops are open-fronted, for instance, and consist of one room on the street level. There are no multiple stores whatsoever, but tin shops and material shops and basket-work shops and silver shops and gold shops and grocers shops and chemists. If you want to buy a dress you go to the street where all the shops sell materials and have them stacked out on the pavement so that you can get a good look at them. When you have bargained for, and bought, what you want, you take your length of material to a dressmaker and hope that he or she won't make a hopeless mess of it. The gold and silver and grocers and chemists and bookshops mostly have glass show-windows on either side of the wide entrance which is kept open all day long, but the whole effect is of shop life being there on the pavement for you to take part in if you want to, whereas in England you definitely have to go into a shop. The streets are rather scruffy and dirty by English standards but you don't very often see scruffy or dirty-looking people. The women mostly wear freshly washed and ironed blouses and skirts or sarongs (long pieces of material which are wrapped round the body to look like a long skirt) and the men may have on rather crumpled looking trousers but their shirts look spruce and clean. It's difficult to look really smart for very long in Bangkok because the sweaty dampness takes the starched look out of the nattiest garment very quickly.

That's all for now, chaps, but before I forget I must add to the little piece about Jill that she has a good friend at school called Caroline Harvey who has had her to stay with her for three weekends, including half-term.

Much love to yourself & all the family, Averin

9th July: "A Thai woman is worth two Thai men!"

British Embassy,
Bangkok,
Thailand.

July 9th, 1957

Dear Everybody,

We've been having a fairly quiet week, socially. Only once out to lunch, once out to dinner, one cocktail party (helping to celebrate the Philippine national day on July 4th) and once to the cinema with friends. Yes, very quiet!! The Philippine party was an enormously crowded affair. After we had drunk all the suitable toasts, members of the Philippine embassy and community danced some of their national dances – somewhat Spanish affairs, and some of them very sedate. They all wore their national dress which sounds quite exciting but in fact the women's simply consisted of long evening dresses with short sleeves starched and standing up from the shoulder, while the men wore hand-embroidered loose shirts over their ordinary trousers.

In her letter Mummy asks some searching questions, including one about the position of women in Thailand compared with ours. I'm not sure I'm in a position to answer this yet but I'll do my best. You have to look at it historically because until 1932 there was an absolute monarchy in Thailand. The king was looked upon as a holy person and everybody had to prostrate themselves before him. In the same way those of lower rank had to bow and scrape before those of higher rank, and this went on all the way through Thai society. In those days polygamy was the thing for those who could afford it and King Chulalongkhorn, for example, the grandfather of the present king (and of Prince Chula in England) had 36 wives and 32 sons and 44 daughters. The wives could never get a divorce, even when they'd been passed over, and the princesses could only marry men of equal rank, of which there were never enough to go round, so the palace was always full of women, married or unmarried, who had a very limited life. This state of affairs must have affected the attitude towards women throughout Thai society, but they never lived the harem life that Moslem women still sometimes do, with veils and things.

Then came 1932, when the King was asked to delegate his ruling powers to a people's government, which he did, and the king is now just a figurehead. Since then all sorts of ideals have been floating round and some of them have been put into action. There have been great educational programmes; schooling is now compulsory for everybody, boys and girls; there are free government schools and all university education is free, except that students have to buy their own books and pay for their own medical treatment. With all this education the views on polygamy have changed and it has been made illegal, and the educated women, at least, are all for enforcing its illegality. They have equal voting rights with men and all the professions are open to them. In fact as students the girls are usually more industrious than the boys and often more intelligent and I've heard people say that as far as personality and integrity go, a Thai woman is worth two Thai men!

Of course, 25 years is a very short time for a revolution to have been going and lots of ideals still only exist as theories or on paper. For instance, this compulsory education. In point of fact there aren't nearly enough schools to go round and there are a great many children still who will never get to school at all. Others have to leave when they're nine. Some of them go to work in factories at that age and some are employed as bus conductors! And then again, the university has a great many faculties and trains people to be this and that, and those who can afford it send their children to American and British universities, but when they are trained there aren't nearly enough jobs to go round. I heard of one fully qualified engineer for whom there were no civil engineering opportunities in Thailand. There is, of course, a great need for good roads, but all government officials are so busy trying to make themselves rich that they overlook a great many of their country's needs and such good roads as there are have been built (and paid for) by the Americans. By our standards a great many things are topsy-turvey. The police are badly paid (they get about £7 a month) and have to work long hours, so who can blame them if they accept bribes in order to increase their income? One colonel in the police force is on the racing committee of the Sports Club. He owns a horse or two and it's well known that he's up to all the tricks of doping. The Thais themselves talk about these things openly and deplore the corruption, whilst practising every known and possible form of corruption themselves, of course. How else to live?

All this sounds very deplorable, yet it's quite wrong to compare their way of life with ours because we have our traditional way of looking at things and they have theirs, and that's how life is lived out here. On the whole Thais are charming, friendly, hospitable people and in this at least they surpass the Egyptians, for example, who were just as corrupt and had very little to commend them as individuals.

Mummy also asks how I get on with my class of social welfare workers. I find them more difficult to teach than the university students because they're most of them a good deal older and some have forgotten what English they knew and others don't seem to have learnt much at all and yet others understand and speak quite a lot. I find it very difficult finding a level that caters for all of them. Yet they must learn English because the Social Welfare department has only existed for two years and there are no Thai textbooks on the subject so they have to use British or American textbooks. There are four women in the class and about 18 men and I must confess the women are better at English though some of the men try very hard! Teaching people individually is much easier than teaching a class because you can draw the individual into some sort of conversation whereas in a class if you ask a question there's a deathly silence and you get the feeling you might be talking double Dutch for all they understand.

[Handwritten note to Margaret]

I can't really talk to Mummy & Dai freely on the subject of women here. In point of fact they're a much discussed topic of conversation, especially among British men, who seem to think there's something particularly luscious about them! Anyway, with Thai men there's no doubt that sex is the main theme in their lives, and though they marry & have families they certainly indulge in a lot of promiscuous living as well, & with no birth control & polygamy now illegal one imagines there must be a lot of illegitimate children about and the Social Welfare dept. has come into existence none too soon.

I hear from Mummy that you're doing a spot of medicine & Mudge has left you. I hope you'll enjoy it & not feel too hard-worked.

Love to you all, Averin

NOTES
Margaret's husband Stuart was a G.P. and ran his surgery in their house in Wallington, Surrey. Mudge (Muriel Fletcher) was for a time the receptionist there.

9th July (2): "An enormous swimming pool"

British Embassy,
Bangkok,
Thailand.

July 9th, 1957

My darling Ann and Michael,

July 4th was the Philippine National Day (the same sort of thing as our Queen's birthday) and the Philippine Embassy gave an enormous cocktail party for all the members of the diplomatic corps and Thai high society. This included us and we went along to the Ratanakosin Hotel and after a while everybody was silent and the Philippine ambassador proposed the toast of his country, the band played their national anthem and we all drank their health. Then he proposed the health of His Majesty the King of Thailand, the band played the Thai national anthem, and we drank to the king of Thailand. Everybody thought that was that and started chatting again, but we suddenly realised another national anthem was being played so we looked very solemn and attentive again. I didn't know whose national anthem it was but Daddy explained afterwards that it was "The Stars and Stripes" and that July 4th was American Independence Day as well! All very confusing.

We've joined the Bangkok sporting club which is a place where you can play almost every game you can think of: golf, cricket, rugger, tennis, badminton, billiards, chess, squash – those are the only ones I can think of at the moment. There's also an enormous swimming pool where you will be able to enjoy yourselves when you come. The joy about swimming here is that you never feel cold, either in the water or out of it and you can spend hours popping in and out of the pool without a grown-up saying, "You're shivering, darling. You simply must go and get dressed!" I've only been once to the pool so far but I enjoyed that very much.

We go to church most Sundays. The church is fairly like an ordinary church – about the size of St. Michael's – except that along both sides instead of windows it has a whole lot of doors which are kept wide open during the service to help keep it cool. There are also ceiling fans which hang from the roof on supports about 15 feet long and are worked by electricity. There's one stained glass window over the altar at the East end. The choir consists of men and women who wear blue cassocks under their white surplices, and the women wear blue square soft hats as well. They sing very energetically but I guess the standard is not quite up to New College, Oxford. I don't think the organist uses the pedals much (not being quite so expert as Mr. Meredith Davies) and the organ is kept going with a hand-bellows worked by a young Thai.

NOTES
Meredith Davies was the choir master at New College in Oxford from 1956-1958. This was where Michael was a chorister from 1956-1961.

16th July: "Geoff and I motored in the new car to Ayuthia"

Bangkok.

July 16th, 1957

Dear Everyone,

My poor typewriter suffered considerably on the sea-journey to Singapore, in fact it ceased to function altogether and I handed it to the purser who did his worst with it and then handed it to the chief engineer, who took it to pieces and lost several vital parts when putting it together again. In Singapore I took it to the Royal agents who tried to persuade me to buy a new one of twenty pounds. However I wouldn't, so they mended mine for just over one pound, and it worked again but not quite so well as previously. Now I have the chance to borrow 'indefinitely' an Olivetti Lettera 22 which is a very handsome machine and infinitely superior to mine, but I haven't quite got the hang of it yet, and when I have been touch-typing gaily for some little time I remember that some numbers and punctuation marks are not quite in the same place as on my typewriter, and the result is somewhat unintelligible. So please forgive any irregularities you may notice. I'm doing my best. I type so badly anyway that you probably won't notice any difference between this and other letters.

On Sunday Geoff and I motored in the new car to Ayuthia, the ancient capital of Thailand. It's about one and a half hours trip from Bangkok, all along a very flat road through very flat countryside and we grew quite excited when we saw the vague outline of one hill on the very far horizon. There were canals on either side of the road for most of the way and lots of domestic buffalos either standing in them or lying down in them with only their noses and the tips of their horns showing. Better still (for the buffalos) some of them were lying submerged in deep hollows of mud which they seemed to have wallowed out for themselves. When they emerged from these in a sucking, squelchy manner, they were shiny and slimy and probably very happy. Most of the buffalos who were standing up, either in the canals or grazing in nearby fields had men or women or boys or girls sitting on their backs and I think their job was to see that the buffalos didn't stray too far from the homestead. If you ever get tired of that Conservative club or the Library, Dai, why not come out here and try sitting on a buffalo? It seems to be a day-long occupation and there were quite a lot of grandfathers doing it, judging from their age. You'd have to wear black cotton trousers and a navy blue cotton shirt (hanging outside) and a large, high, straw hat, and you'd look pretty unkempt, but I must say all these people seemed contented and well-fed. Perhaps Aunty Gran could have a go at it too when she wasn't cooking the rice for supper or doing a spot of hoeing in the paddy-field or giving herself a good scrub down standing in the canal and wearing a sarong!

Well, we arrived at last in Ayuthia – at least, we imagined it was Ayuthia because there were one or two very delapidated and obviously old ruins about. We couldn't really tell because almost all the signposts were in Thai – and the first building we visited was a large and imposing green one with warlike figures round the top which we thought must be a museum but this turned out to be a mistake and I think it was only the town hall. We didn't really know which ruin to visit first and they were all so very scattered about but we soon found a clean-looking outdoor café and there we sat down to perpend and to consume beer and orange fizz. All the Thais there smiled benignly upon us and two young men came over and tried very hard to practise their limited knowledge of English upon us. They told us that we were on an iceland and after a while we realised that they meant island and tried without much success to improve their pronunciation of the word. They wanted to show us round but we had some sandwiches to eat so we excused ourselves and Geoff gave them his card and told them to be sure to come and call on us whenever they came here. After that we drove away and sat in the car to eat our lunch and as soon as we had started two more young men came up and asked if they could act as our guides for us. We said they could when we had finished eating so they stood and watched us and we tried to be as quick as possible, forcing hunks of ham sandwiches down our throats and scalding hot coffee. We were quite grateful to these young men because they were able to show us where the public conveniences were. If you can't read Thai script and don't know the Thai words for Men and Women anyway this can be quite a problem. In the ladies all the doors were locked up (and no provision made for the equivalent of pennies) and I was wondering what to do when two small boys dashed up on bicycles and one of them produced a bunch of keys and unlocked a door and waved me in with great ceremony. So that was all right.

One of our young men was a student at a teacher's training college and desperately keen to communicate with us in English so we did our best to help him in return for his guiding services. They took us first to a Jeddi, or monument, a huge tall white affair which looked rather like the leaning tower of Pisa in that it leaned, and it also looked suspiciously modern. But we realised from a picture in the young man's guide book that this was a very ancient monument which had been renovated and covered over with shiny white concrete. We climbed up the very steep steps (and it was a VERY, exceptionally hot day) and enjoyed a fairly cool breeze while we gazed over the far countryside. After this the young men took us around a bit more but it was so hot we soon got exhausted and said we must go home. They were deeply disappointed but Geoff gave them his card and told them to be sure to come and call on us whenever they came here.

Perhaps I should become historical at this point and explain that Ayuthia was the capital of Thailand until about 200 years ago, when the Burmese sacked it and reduced it to such a shambles that the king lost heart and decided to start again elsewhere. He picked on Bangkok, a tiny village, for his new capital, so you see Bangkok is a comparatively new city and its wats and things that you visit are interesting but not ancient. The Burmese didn't manage to stay in Thailand, which has never really been conquered and ruled by any outsider, and this makes it different from most other countries in the Far East.

Ruins at Ayuthia

On the way home from Ayuthia we passed the airport and dropped in to its air-conditioned dining-room for a drink. Many Thais and others go there for a drink or a meal as it's half-an-hour's drive out from Bangkok and makes a change, and the children can play around and watch the aeroplanes. There isn't nearly such a crowd there as you get at London airport and landings and taking-offs aren't very frequent but just frequent enough to keep one's interest going. And now I've remembered that all this happened on Saturday, not Sunday, because on Sunday morning we took a friend who was flying to Hong Kong to the airport and drank coffee and watched more planes. And on Sunday evening we went to church. The parson was mouldy after a relapse of flu so the service was taken by an educated member of the choir who really did it very well and got all his responses right, and the parson only preached the sermon, and Geoff took round the collection bag and got that right too.

MICHAEL RICHARD HINTON

[Handwritten note to Margaret]

The holidays will be starting almost as soon as you get this. I hope Michael will behave himself. How on earth are you going to help Stuart and everything as well?

Much love from Averin

23rd July: "Rather like a bird's nest"

British Embassy,
Bangkok.

July 23rd, 1957

Dear Everybody,

Great consternation and flap-doodle to-day because the bag day has suddenly been changed from Friday to Tuesday, and instead of having a whole morning to write to you, with odd free evenings to add little bits, I've got to write to the whole jolly lot of you, children's editions an' all, in 2 and a half hours (just discovered this typewriter, with all its §s and +s and ùs and whatnot, hasn't got any fractions).

Yesterday evening we were invited to dinner with Mr. Bawa, first secretary in the Indian Embassy. He's a Sikh (at least, Geoffrey says he is; I'm not quite sure what a Sikh is) and always wears a white turban and has a great deal of black curly beard which goes on up his cheeks, in front of his ears, and disappears underneath the turban. The beard is encased in a black net which also disappears beneath the turban, so you can't quite see how it's kept in place, and the whole thing looks rather like a bird's nest.

Well, we went along to Mr. & Madame Bawa's house, and there she was on the doorstep, very fat and matronly, clad in a beautiful blue sari (if you want to know the difference between a sari and a sarong you must look them up in your dictionaries), and beside her was their eldest daughter, a slim 20-year-old also clad in a blue sari with gold and red bands round the bottom, and Mr. Bawa came out to greet us, clad in a white drill suit, white turban – and beard. There was also evidence of several younger Bawas, young Bawa noises coming from the balcony over our heads and not-so-young Bawa faces peeping out of doorways and so on, but these Bawas didn't make any formal appearance.

We were taken into the sitting-room and as this was a buffet dinner there were about 13 of us altogether, 2 men from Air India, a UNO Indian and his wife, an Australian counsellor and his wife, a Laotian (from Laos which used to be part of French Indo-China but is now a country in its own right on the eastern border of Thailand), an Indonesian and his wife and, the guest of the evening, the Indian ambassador and his two very charming daughters and son. The two daughters wore saris and the Indonesian lady wore her national costume, a sort of sarong with a red silk tight-fitting blouse and a rose stuck into the back of her hair.

It looked to me as if it would be an interesting evening, but after we had been sipping our tomato juices or whisky-sodas for a while the men gradually began to drift away into the lounge-hall, and there we ladies were, left to our own devices, and there we stayed for the rest of the evening. Well, we did pass through the hall to the dining room to help ourselves to delicious dishes of rice and meats and fish and vegetables cooked in the Indian manner (but not curried) but then we passed back into our sitting-room with a purdah of mosquito netting between us and the men. However, it was quite fun. All the Indian ladies spoke English because, as perhaps you know, many different languages are spoken in India and they have to use English as their common language. Madame Bawa was the only one who didn't really speak much English so the ambassador's daughters talked to her in Hindi. Miss Bawa spoke very fluent English but I couldn't understand it. She seemed to be telling me that it was very dull to have passed through College and then to have to come and live a life of leisure in Bangkok, and papa was very tiresome because he insisted on her wearing a sari here, whereas at home in India she and all her co-students wear European dress. However, papa did relent enough to allow her to wear jeans in the house when nobody was about. This young lady said very much more to me, but this, I think, was the gist of the matter, and I had to concentrate very hard to get that much.

When it was time to go home the ambassador's daughters tried to attract their father's attention but he was deeply engrossed in lecturing to the men, who were seated in a circle round him, paying reverend attention and sometimes nodding their heads, but never shaking them. Geoffrey told me afterwards that the subject was the Kashmir question (don't worry children; I don't know what it is either) so I was quite glad that we had been left to ourselves to discuss such cultured subjects as Indian dancing, to finger each other's clothes and admire them, to tell each other how many children we had and to admit how bored, or boast how busy, we were. At last, after much gesticulation on the part of the ambassador's elder daughter and giggling from the rest of us, the ambassador's attention was at last caught, the senior guest was borne away by his family and the rest of us followed at a respectful distance.

On Sunday morning Geoffrey and I motored to Nakorn Pathom, a town about 35 miles to the east of Bangkok. To get there we had to go over the only bridge over the river on which Bangkok stands (called the Menam Chao Phya) and there was a grand old bottleneck of traffic there, but once we were over it the going was quite easy, except that the surface of this main road to the east was in a deplorable condition and full of bumps. The main attraction in Nakorn Pathom is an enormous golden Jeddi, or Buddhist monument, for those who don't know, which the guide book says dates back to the 2nd century B.C. It also seemed to be used as a monastery for Buddhist priests and there were various chapels with statue representations of Buddha lying down and preaching to admirers or sitting up and preaching. Thai visitors knelt down and prayed in these chapels and stuck burning joss sticks into the sand in front of Buddha or stuck bits of gold leaf onto his body, which is a good thing to do if you want things to go well with you. Incidentally I've discovered that Buddhists don't actually worship Buddha who was only a man with no claim to deity. Also the Buddhists don't believe in God but in the spiritual unity of the whole universe. When the lesser-educated say their prayers, however, they find it easier to worship one particular person so they address themselves to the statue of Buddha. This is a Bad Thing in the eyes of the authorities but nothing much can be done about it.

Phra Pathom Chedi at Nakorn Pathom, 57 km west of Bangkok

Anyway, Geoffrey and I had a very pleasant half-hour wandering round the Jeddi which was cool and shaded, and then we had to beetle back as fast as the pot-holes would let us to a late lunch at 2 o'clock.

Must stop now and write to Michael and Jill. Many thanks, Mummy, for your letter of July 13th, with news up to your visit to Oxford, and Florence, for your letter of the 17th, with news of the visit and after. Jill sent me four snap-shots of herself and friend Caroline sitting on the sea-shore, Jill with one front tooth evidently missing and Caroline with hardly any front teeth at all. Not exactly an age for photography! But of course it was lovely to get the snaps. She also spent a week-end with the three children of a Dr. Barnado who go to her school. The father is a relation of the Dr. Barnado.

Much love to all of you, *Averin*

29th July: "Very uncomfortable and sinful"

British Embassy,
Bangkok,
Thailand.

July #0th, 1ç(è

(all in code, of course!)

Dear Everyone,

This week my diary-calendar's got all sorts of odd things written down among the cocktail parties and what-not. For instance, it says that Bernards Heath term ends on the 26th, and besides saying that the High School ends on the 25th it says that the next High School term is from the 19th September till the 19th December and that their half term will be on November 1st. Since none of this concerns any of us any more it seems rather silly to have it all written down! However, we thought of Ann breaking up on the 25th and setting off for Weston with Noëlle and Gillian, and on the 26th at 4.30 p.m. (our time) we thought of Jill starting at 10.30 a.m. (her time) on her first train journey all by herself. And to-morrow we'll be thinking of Michael having his sports day (weather permitting) and then starting on his first train journey all by himself to Paddington. It's just pouring with rain here to-day and everything's saturated, but this is a Good Thing as so far the rainy season's been exceptionally dry and the rice crop has suffered and the country people are very worried.

We haven't really done anything very exciting this week. Yesterday we went to church and heard a very good, ordinary-language sermon by the new Archbishop of Capetown. He was in the middle of a 3-months world tour when he was suddenly told of his appointment so he's had to cut down the tour to 3 weeks and we're quite lucky to have had him in Bangkok. He preached a sermon which ended up with the apartheid problem but started off with much more general implications which made you feel very uncomfortable and sinful and rather relieved in the end to think that perhaps the South African Whites were a little bit more sinful (but not much). After the service some of us went to the parsonage and had a chat with him. In the afternoon we went to a christening and the Archbishop turned up for that as well, and came to the tea-party afterwards – a sumptuous spread of cucumber and paste sandwiches and asparagus rolls and finally the cake, a dundee cake sent specially by bag from England and elaborately iced here. There were cups of tea, of course, and while we were drinking them there were loud popping noises in the background and presently the champagne flowed and we drank to the health of Alison Clare Spankie, who incidentally had yelled throughout the service but was now happily drinking her own health from a bottle of deliciously refreshing cold water.

This was our second christening running. On Saturday a 3½ months old gentleman called Robert Moncrieff Curwen was brought to the font having travelled all the way from Vien-tiane (capital of Laos) for that purpose. His mother is a Burmese, a charming person called Noon, who wore a sarong for the occasion, and his father was a friend of Geoff's in London. Robert behaved himself very well during the ceremony and didn't cry at all.

Sam See and her mother have somewhat fallen from grace this week as I had to line them up and tell them, with Cookie acting as interpreter, that although we are not supposed to supply them with food Geoff and I were apparently consuming more butter than our whole family eats in England (and remember we never have afternoon tea) and that Geoff's pot of honey, which normally lasts for weeks and weeks at home, was being finished off at the rate of one in 8 days here! Since a pot of honey costs just over 8s. in Bangkok we were distinctly peeved about this. Sam See and her mum looked suitably hang-doggish and didn't deny their guilt. They went round the house looking very glum all that day but next day they were as bright and bobbish as ever, though perhaps a little more respectful and eager to please than usual. Throughout the rebuking interview Cookie looked sad and smug. Little does he know that as soon as I've learned enough Thai I shall be off to market, comparing prices with the prices he writes down in his market book! This is the sort of game which Geoff and I learnt to play in Egypt and it must show you only too well that there is another side to the luxury of having so many servants.

Geoff is now having two Thai lessons a week and I have one. A lady comes to the house to instruct us. Geoff is learning the script as well but it's quite enough for me to try and cope with the language alone. What with the five different tones it's almost a matter of singing at first but later on one learns to bring the thing down to a speaking level. I'm better at forgetting than remembering what I've been taught and spend hours chanting away to myself and then when I want to say some quite simple phrase to someone no words flow at all. Still, I've only had three lessons so I suppose it's early days yet.

Love to everyone – Averin

NOTES

Robert Moncrieff Curwen was the infant son of Christopher Curwen, an MI6 colleague of Geoffrey's who became head of MI6 from 1985 to 1989.

Alison Clare Spankie was the infant daughter of Douglas and Jane Spankie. Douglas was a 2nd Secretary at the British Embassy and an MI6 colleague of Geoffrey's.

Bernards Heath was the infants' school that Jill had been to when Averin and Geoffrey lived in St Albans. High School refers to the St Albans High School for Girls, which Ann attended before going to Cheltenham Ladies College.

5th August: "We've been rather gay this week"

British Embassy,
Bangkok,
Thailand.

August 5th, 1957.

Dear Everybody,

(And this really does mean everybody, children and all. I'm rather pushed for time this week because I've given my university students a test which means I've got 360 papers to correct and it's taking up all my spare moments)...

I have lots of nice letters to thank you all for. One from Jill told us she arrived at Paddington safely after a "lovely ride on the train" and we also got her report from Mrs. Tomlinson which is a wonderful affair full of "goods" and "very goods" and "excellents" and telling us that she got 53 red marks last term and no black marks and that she was first in her form. Then there was a letter from Michael with lots of sporting details and all about a "boy called Bullwinkle" who broke a record, though what record he broke we don't quite know. Granny tells us all about Ann's departure to Weston-Super-Mare and Jill's arrival at St. Albans and Auntie Gran paints a sad picture of Granpa walking all the way down into Oxford from Headington in the morning and home again at night during the bus strike. But we hope that's all over now as we read in our paper a few days ago that the bus strike had ended. No news from Ann on her holiday so far, but that probably means she's far too busy having a good time to write. Thank you, everybody, for all your letters. We always read them over at least six times each (or at any rate I do; probably Geoff drinks in their contents at a single glance) and are very happy to know about what you're all up to.

We've been rather gay this week, and on two evenings running we went to cocktail parties and then on to dinner parties afterwards. The first cocktail party was given by a Thai newspaper woman called Madame S. na Ranong and was held as a farewell gesture to some gentleman in the Indonesian Embassy. Geoffrey wandered round discussing important matters with diplomats and officials but I joined a group of women who were sitting down (and sitting down is a rare luxury at a cokctail party!). They were the two daughters of the Indian ambassador, the wife of the Soviet chargé d'affaires, the wife of a German diplomat and the daughter of an Italian diplomat. We got along very happily together, English of course being the common language. How fortunate we are that English is the international language! This cocktail party was given at the Ratanakosin Hotel, commonly known as the Rat, and as the ladies and I were sitting talking the Indian ambassador's elder daughter suddenly put her hand on my knee and said in a quiet voice, "Do you see what I can see?" and when I looked, there was a rat walking across the floor! At least, we thought it was a rat. It looked like a rat that had lost its tail.

After this cocktail party we went to dinner in the counsellor's house in the British Embassy compound where we were bidden to say farewell to a member of our own Embassy. There were about 15 guests there, some Thais and some British - and the Wongs, who of course are Chinese but are now naturalised British. The counsellor is a bachelor but his house is enormous and his dining-room table is a vast affair which accommodated our large number easily. In the lobby outside the dining-room there was a plan showing our places at table so when we had studied this we knew exactly where we should sit. I was between Mr. Wong and the British Military Attaché, a jolly colonel with a red face and a handlebar moustache, while Geoffrey was between a Thai government official and Mrs. Wong. We drank white wine with the fish and red wine with the roast beef, and then with the sweet came champagne, with which we toasted the health of the departing diplomat.

After coffee we ladies departed upstairs to powder our noses and went into an enormous guest bedroom which had a sort of cage made of mosquito mesh in the middle, and in that was a rather small-looking single bed. One of the Thais, a woman of about 25, spoke very good English and when I asked her about this she said she had spent many years in England and had in fact been a Cheltenham Lady! So we had a long old-school gossip and a good giggle together because we had both disliked Miss Popham. This Thai lady is a niece of the Thai queen and therefore a rather high-society dame.

I must pause in the middle of this to say that Geoffrey has just come home with three more letters, one from Granpa saying that Michael won second prize for throwing the cricket ball, was top of his form, had 12 stars and no stripes, and one from Ann which is full of riding lessons and frolicksome horses down in Weston, and one from Granny to Geoffrey, a more sober document, going into the cost of the riding lessons and also saying that Ann had honours in all subjects at school except two. What have we done to deserve three such extraordinary children? If there ever comes a day when one of them is third or fourth in form we shall probably be very affronted, though I imagine that Ann may become a little unhitched at Cheltenham, where all the ladies are so very intelligent!

Our second cocktail party this week was given by the British Naval Attaché to give good wishes to Commodore Aghai Sitakalin who is going to be Thai Naval Attaché in London. It was given at Commander and Mrs. Andrew's house and every now and then I noticed a small boy clad in white shirt and trousers darting in and out among the guests in a crouching position. This, I think, must have been Master Andrew, who was perhaps playing Red Indians or was some gallant soldier carrying dispatches through the enemy lines at great personal risk to himself. Whatever he was, he did it very silently and I'm sure a great many of the guests didn't notice him.

The second dinner party was given by a Lt. Colonel in the Thai police. We were bidden to an address called the Little Home Bakery which sounded odd because it was so English, and we had quite a lot of difficulty in finding it. It was in a fairly squalid street (but most Bangkok streets are squalid) among a lot of Chinese shops but when we had driven through the main gates we found ourselves in a quiet and peaceful compound of pleasant wooden houses. The owner of this compound is married to a Filipino woman whose family have a bakery in Manila and who decided to start a bakery of her own in Bangkok. They make bread and cakes and pastries and have just built a new biscuit factory, and it was on the flat roof of this that our party was held. There were several Thai police there and several Americans and their wives and just us two Britishers. We all sat round and talked and drank and ate savoury pastries for a long time, and then at about 10 o'clock we had a buffet supper consisting of rice and hot curry and pork and heart and lobster and salad, all spread out on an enormous table for us to help ourselves. When we had filled ourselves up with this a great many fruits were brought round so we stuffed a few of these into such odd corners as we had left, but then came ice creams, and of course we had to eat these so as not to give offence, and then came cakes and pastries, and of course we had to eat these because they had been made by the Little Home Bakery. After this we sat in a replete and rather somnolent manner, making great efforts to chat brightly until about midnight. It was rather a sticky party because not all the Thais wanted to talk to us (presumably because they didn't speak English well) but we and the Americans felt we had to try to talk to them because it would have been rude just to sit talking to each other.

Yesterday, Sunday, Geoffrey and I went to church at 10 o'clock and then set off with a lunch picnic for Bangpa-in, the summer residence of past Thai kings. It was built originally by King Chulalongkhorn (the king in Anna and the King of Siam and The King and I) and has a most extraordinary mixture of architecture in it. King Chulalongkhorn was the first Thai king to be interested in Western culture and in this enormous park there is a European residence built in the style of Versailles, a Buddhist temple built to look like a Christian church, a hot water storage that looks like a mediaeval castle, a cold water storage that looks like a light-house, a bridge with Venuses and other Grecian ladies standing on its parapet and two memorials to one of Chulalongkhorn's wives and her children, one with sculpted busts of them all and the other with two inscriptions, one in Thai and the other in very amateurish English. This poor wife and her children were drowned when a royal barge overturned in the river and as it was forbidden for any person to touch a royal personage (penalty for so-doing was death) they were just left to drown.

Averin & Geoffrey at Bang Pa-In

Besides all these Europeanish things there is a Thai pagoda standing in the middle of a lake, several Thai houses which were the dwellings of concubines and an enormous Chinese residence which we were taken over by a guide. We had to take our shoes off at the entrance and then we went straight into the throne room which had a floor made up of coloured porcelain tiles and had one or two chairs made of dark wood studded most beautifully with mother-of-pearl. In fact all the furniture in the building was made in this Chinese style and there were Chinese vases and crockery in cupboards here and there. On one side of the room, at the top of about six stairs, was the king's throne, with a marble symbol in front of it, and it was on this that you had to bump your head when you had an audience with the king and prostrated yourself in front of him. Immediately behind the throne was the council chamber, with a raised seat for the king and various chairs and tables set about for his counsellors. Behind this again were several small bedrooms for favoured concubines and a European bathroom complete with bathtub fitted with taps, a wash-basin and a W.C. The mod. cons. were installed by King Mongkut, the son of Chullalongkorn. Upstairs there were two bedrooms, one for the King and one for the Queen (the first wife was always the Queen and the others were just 'wives'), another European bathroom, a room with a sort of shrine in it and a living room with an enormous golden writing desk - a kind of drawing-room, I suppose. These upstairs rooms were very lofty but their wooden partitions were only about ten feet high, allowing for free circulation of air.

We found this all very interesting, as you can imagine. Unfortunately the present king isn't very interested in Bangpa-in and prefers to spend his holidays at Hua Hin, a modern seaside resort, so the old place is rather neglected and looks very dilapidated in parts.

On our way back to Bangkok we could see a great storm brewing. There was a strong wind blowing across the road and buses and lorries had stopped to put huge tarpaulins on their loads of baskets or whatever it was they were carrying. All bus luggage is put on the roof and some of them looked comically top-heavy. When we drove into the rain we could hardly see where we were going, it was so fierce. We stopped off at the airport for a while but there wasn't much doing as it was a Sunday. The rain cleared up for a bit but it started again as soon as we started on our last lap and we arrived in a deluge and thunder storm to find the house surrounded by a lake (it's raised off the ground so this was all right). What wasn't all right was a pool of water in our bedroom, and Som See told us her bedroom was so swamped that she would have to move into a room in Cookie's house for the night. To-day it hasn't rained all day but the ground is still pretty damp and the canals and ditches are all full of muddy, swollen waters.

Geoff is leaving for Singapore tomorrow, for a conference of sorts. He leaves by air at 9.30 a.m. and will be coming back on Sunday morning.

I didn't mean to write such a long letter as this, but somehow it went on and on. Before I stop I must thank Dai for taking Michael all the way to Paddington. It was very feeble of the school, we think, not to have the sports day at a more convenient time, but as most boys do travel by car I suppose it was convenient for them to have the parents on the spot to take them away. And thank you, Mummy, for sending the stamps which arrived by bag. You can send anything by bag that can go by letter-post, but we are only allowed to receive six parcels in a year.

In answer to Florence's question, Mrs. Tomlinson goes away on holiday with her own children for three weeks, but Ann, Michael and Jill are all going down to her at Par on August 25th and will be staying there a fortnight.

Much love from us both to everybody, *Averin*

x x x Mummy & Daddy x x x

NOTES

As Averin confesses in a later letter (9th September) she got her facts wrong about the king in *Anna and the King of Siam* and in the musical *The King and I*. King Mongkut was the King who employed Anna Leonowens, and Chulalongkorn was his son.

Miss Popham was the Principal of Cheltenham Ladies College, the boarding school that Averin and Margaret had both been to, and where Ann would soon be going.

13th August:
"Prowling round the garden"

British Embassy,
Bangkok,
Thailand.

August 13th, 1957.

Dear Everybody,

On Sunday morning I rang up the World Travel Bureau and learned that CPA (Cathay Pacific Airways) Flight No. CX 728 was due to arrive on time at 11 am. so at 10 o'clock the driver and I set forth together in the car for the airport. It only took us 35 minutes to get there, but sometimes when traffic is very bad it takes an hour so we had to allow plenty of time. There were dozens of Thais and Chinese there, indulging in their national pastime of seeing friends off and I sat about and watched them until 11.15 when Geoff's plane came in. He'd had a comfortable trip, much better than the one to Singapore, when the KLM plane he was booked on was 18 hours behind schedule so he had to go on a Burmese Airways aircraft instead. This was a Dakota, and a filthy dirty one at that, and the food supplied was nauseating, and the trip took 6 hours instead of the KLM and CPA 3 and a half because they stopped at Penang on the way. He had a very busy time in Singapore, sitting up and discussing matters until 2 or 3 a.m. every night, so I guess he was quite glad to get back here. We didn't have a holiday on August Bank Holiday but yesterday was the Thai Queen's birthday and we had a holiday then instead, so Geoff didn't have to go into the Embassy and work.

I had quite a busy time while he was away, getting on with my teaching and so forth. If the man of the house is away the wife of a British Embassy official is provided with a nightwatchman so I had a handsome young Indian-Thai prowling round the garden, flashing his torch on imaginary prowlers and burglars. I think he slept on the porch, just by the front door.

On the Tuesday afternoon my class of Social Welfare Workers had asked to be excused their lesson because they wanted to go to the Seminar which is being held on Asian Women's rights, and when I said I'd like to go too they invited me to go along with them. The conference was being held in a rather gorgeous, air-conditioned hall and to me it seemed rather a pity that the hall wasn't better filled. The delegates (from Hong Kong, Nationalist China, Japan, India, Pakistan, Indonesia, Thailand, Burma - and any other Eastern country you can think of) only occupied about the first six rows, and apart from a few school girls and the Social Workers and a few others the rest of the place was empty.

As a matter of fact the whole session was deadly dull because they'd tabulated various statements at previous meetings and spent the entire afternoon haggling over the wording of these. But what did interest me was the interpreting of the speeches. Every chair in the hall was provided with head-phones and by turning a switch it was possible to hear translations in English, Thai or French. Actually all the delegates talked in English, but sometimes I listened to the French translation, which was amazing because the man seemed to be able to speak and listen at the same time. The Thai woman wasn't so professional. She just listened for a time and then gave a summary of what had been said. This wasn't very satisfactory for the Thai listeners-in but the Social Welfare Workers tried to understand the English a lot of the time.

The head of the Social Welfare Department, who organises the class, had asked me very apologetically if I could help her put her speeches into good English and I said I would be delighted to so she came round here on Saturday morning and we spent about three hours on her two speeches. In the afternoon I typed them out for her and she came back in the evening and practised reading them aloud. She made one of the speeches yesterday and I would have liked to go and hear her but wasn't able to get there. The other one's to be on Wednesday morning and I must try to get there for that. As a result of my services, Geoff and I are invited to her tenth wedding anniversary celebrations on August 25th. She was very anxious lest Geoff as a diplomat should consider himself too elevated for their company, though she explained that her husband was a lecturer in engineering at the University, and that although they weren't aristocratic they were well-educated and sober people. So I told her that we too were of common, middle-class stock and would be only too pleased to break away from diplomatic circles for a change.

As you can imagine, as a result of Saturday's session there's very little I don't know about the position of women in Thailand, from the richest to the poorest. I know something about their numerous women's voluntary social organisations and about their attempts to raise the standard of living in the poorest homes. They have to educate the people in elementary matters like sanitation and cleanliness and good house-building before they start on anything else, so it seems they have a long, long road ahead of them before these women are ready to make a contribution to local or any other sort of government (which is the aim of the seminar).

When Geoff was in Singapore he bought me a watch, which I needed very badly (I can't remember what happened to the one Mummy gave me in England but I think the watchmonger said it wasn't worth mending) and also a thing called a pocket-viewer, which is a small, folded thing for looking at colour transparencies through a magnifying glass. I've just got back my first lot of colour transparencies and I'm quite thrilled with the results. The colours are so natural, and when you look at the pictures through the viewer they somehow look three-dimensional too. The one of Geoff in his car has come out very well, and the one of Cookie in his samlor too, so I must get them reprinted in black and white and send them off to you all.

No letters from anyone this week except Mummy but some may have come in yesterday during the holiday.

Much love to you all, *Averin*

[Handwritten note to Margaret]

I was glad to hear from Mummy that you all enjoyed your holiday in Italy. Fancy camping and <u>enjoying</u> *it! I'm sure I couldn't. But it must have been fun going to Italy.*

I can hear Stuart snorting at my "indigestion". It was only that I ate two most delicious cocktail onions perched on squares of cheese and speared with tooth-picks. Onions always disagree with me but sometimes I can't resist them.

So far we've both kept pretty well - touch wood. Geoffrey's athlete's foot became so fungoid that it looked as if large portions of flesh were rotting away so he took it to a doctor who prescribed powders and ointments which healed it and kept it at bay. Doctors are madly expensive (70 baht, or £1/4/4 for a short visit to the surgery, 150 baht if they come to your house) but we get it refunded on the National Health. How do these prices compare with doctors' fees in England? People sometimes ask me and I just don't know.

I never gave you a birthday present so I'm enclosing a cheque with which I hope you can buy something. As I told Mummy, I'm going to try to devise some means of getting Christmas presents home to you all. I know someone who's going home in October so I may send the things with her sea luggage. I don't quite know how to cope with the customs but I dare say something can be managed.

Much love from Averin.

13th August (2): " I felt a very important personage"

British Embassy,
Bangkok.

August 13th 1957.

My darling Mummy,

While Geoff was away last week I went to a buffet supper given by the head of the British Council (Robert the Bruce) in honour of a British medical man called Professor C.A. Wells who was passing through Bangkok on his way to Australia. Somebody said this chap came from Liverpool so I told him I was born there and he asked what my maiden name was. I said Macalister and he said not a relation of THE Macalister of the Royal Southern Hospital and I said but yes, a daughter and he, looking closely at me, said but that surely was impossible and I, explaining the generations, said it was not only possible but true. He seemed very delighted with all this because he, too, was on the staff of the Royal Southern, from 1926 till 1945.

While we were talking I happened to mention Daddy's memoires and he said who were the publishers and I explained that they hadn't been published. He was very anxious to get hold of them for the Liverpool Medical Institute and when I said they were a bit woolly in parts he said he didn't mind if every word was mis-spelt, it was the sort of document they wanted as a contribution towards the medical history of Liverpool. At first he said that you should write to the Liverpool Medical Institute about it but afterwards he said it would be still better if you wrote to himself. He didn't give me an address, and of course I don't know if you want to part with the memoires, but if you would like to write to him I can probably get his address from the Bruces. He's only going to Australia on a lecturing tour.

The eminent Thai doctors and surgeons at this gathering had given him an illustrated book about one of the Thai hospitals as a souvenir of his visit to Bangkok, and he asked all of us present at the party to sign our names in the front of this book, and when I signed mine he insisted that I should put née Macalister after it. And when I said goodbye to him he put his hands on my shoulders and said, "Well, goodbye, Macalister; this has been a very happy day!"

Really, I felt a very important personage!

Thank you very much for your letter of July 28th. You're giving Jill a very happy time, I can see, and I can imagine it's quite an effort for you to fit in a visit to a swimming pool every morning with her and Jane. I hope she's rewarding you for your troubles with affection and considerate behaviour, and not providing you with too many clothes to wash. I would very much like to have the photo of her school mates; I should pop it in the bag with Ann's school reports etc.

Miriam's address is EERIKINKATU 26.A.2., Helsinki, Finland. When you write you might ask if she got an airmail letter from me. After the failure of Geoff's letter to reach Ann I'm wondering if others have gone astray, though Heracles got one from Geoff in Australia. Geoff sent the children post cards from Singapore and will be glad to know that they arrived safely.

I'm enclosing a cheque for 57 pounds, which is the total of my earnings for last month and a bit of this! I gave the money to Geoff so he's written the cheque for you, and we wonder if you'll be so kind as to buy premium bonds with it (in my name, presumably).

The best months here as far as climate is concerned are December, January and November (sorry to put them in that order). By November the rains are over and the weather is at its coolest, not too humid and as warm as a good English summer. Would it be possible for you to come immediately after the

Christmas holidays and stay on into February, when it will only just be hotting up? I know November would be pretty hopeless because it's too near Christmas and on the wrong side of it for coming away.

Much love from Averin

NOTES

Averin's father was Dr C. J. Macalister, a consultant physician and paediatrician at Liverpool's Royal Southern Hospital. In 1936 he wrote and published a history of this hospital.

Miriam was from Finland and had worked as au-pair for the Hintons at 9 Avenue Road in St Albans. Averin kept in touch with her all her life.

19th August: "One can't get to know everybody's national anthem"

British Embassy,
Bangkok.

August 19th, 1957

Dear Everybody,

There has been quite a little flutter of political excitement here this week because the President of Vietnam, Ngo Dinh Diem has been paying an official visit. He arrived by air on Thursday and went by special train from the airport to the King's own railway station in Bangkok.

Ngo Dinh Diem, President of Vietnam

So the railway station at the airport and all the bridges under which the train would travel were decorated with Vietnamese and Thai national flags, and there were Thai and Vietnamese flags on sale for children to wave at the president whenever he passed their way. His stay has only been for four days and he's been kept pretty busy during that time doing the sort of things that heads of state usually do on official visits, like laying a wreath on the Thai War Memorial and visiting universities and so forth. It's been reported that he and the king got on well together and exchanged dinner parties and did their best to strengthen cultural ties against that demon, Communist propaganda in Asia. The king at <u>his</u> dinner party broke protocol so far as to escort the president half way down the palace steps, while the President at <u>his</u> dinner party introduced the King to a special soya-bean wine and <u>promised</u> to send him a supply. The only fly in the ointment occurred yesterday when the Prime Minister of Thailand, Pibul Pibulsonggram, who had promised to take the President to Ayuthia, suddenly backed out and sent his son-in-law to take him instead. However, President Diem is a stout fellow and made the best of the son-in-law.

On Saturday evening the Vietnamese Embassy gave a reception in honour of their President and invited representatives from all the diplomatic missions. They have a new Embassy building which they've only been in for a week, so everything looked very shiny and new. It's not a large, specially-built compound like ours but an ordinary private house converted (I think!). Anyway, there we were, the men in black ties and sharkskin jackets and the ladies in long or ballet-length dresses, and at first we were all squashed together rather warmly on a sort of verandah, but then people began to drift into the garden, which was all lit up with coloured lights, and that was much cooler. There was a swimming pool in the garden, with diving boards and all, but nobody succumbed to the temptation to take a quick bathe.

When we first arrived the President wasn't there, but at one point during the evening two Vietnamese were seen to be standing to attention; the band was playing something that might have been a national anthem (the trouble is, one can't get to know everybody's national anthem: there are so many of them) and we guessed the President must be arriving. Some people surged in to

83

shake him by the hand, but we were having a chat in the garden, and by the time we surged the President was just leaving. Geoff swears he caught a glimpse of him before he stepped into his car, but I only saw the back of a lot of people's heads.

Yesterday (Sunday) we went on another of our excursions in the car. This time we took two friends with us, the Pattersons. He's a third secretary in the Embassy, a young chap of about 25, a Cambridge Classics man who can swop classical quotations with Geoff and rave with him over the glories of ancient and modern Greece. His wife is a Swede who must be about 22 and speaks English well.

We went to a place called Kanburi which is twice as far away as Nakorn Patom which we visited a few weeks ago and which I told you about. We stopped for a short while at Nakorn Patom because the Pattersons hadn't been there and they wanted to look at the Pra Cedi (pronounced jeddi) and I took another photograph of Geoff in the car because I've discovered it isn't really suitable to have black-and-white prints made from colour prints. For one thing, it's very expensive because a new negative has to be made from the colour thing, and for another the lighting in the colour transparency has to have been exactly right to make a good black-and-white picture. Of my first 8 pictures, all of which I thought were so exactly right and beautiful, only 2 apparently are worth having printed, and the one of Geoff in the car is not one of them. However, Dai, don't lose heart because black-and-white pictures can be developed and printed in one day in this country and the film in my camera now is black-and-white and as soon as I've finished it I'll be able to send the print off to you.

Kanburi is not a madly interesting place in itself, but it has quite a lot of hills near it, and after the flat plains round Bangkok it's quite a thrill to see a hill. But I must say, during our drive the flat plains looked quite nice because the rice is beginning to grow now and where before the fields were grey and earthy and uninteresting they're now full of light green rice plants standing in ankle-deep water. But to get back to Kanburi we really went there to visit a cemetery which is a memorial to British and Australian and Dutch prisoners of war who died during the building of the Burma to Malaya railway. It's an enormous plot of ground laid out with thousands of small, square uniform stones, each with a brass plaque giving the name of a soldier and his regiment and a suitable text or message suggested by relatives. Everything is very beautifully kept by the War Graves Commission who employ a resident caretaker and numerous Thais to cut the grass and tend the flowers.

Chungkai war cemetry at Kanburi (Kanchanaburi)

We had our lunch picnic at the rest house specially provided for just that in the cemetery, and then the caretaker sent a man with us to a small sort of river port to arrange for us to go up the river by launch to visit another cemetery. We stood about for five or ten minutes while the launch was prepared for us, and watched people washing themselves and their clothes in the muddy water and they watched us, doubtless with amused interest. When the launch was ready we stepped in and arranged ourselves as best we could on the bare but beautifully polished boards, and wished we had the Thai knack of sitting on their haunches. The trip up river took about 25 minutes and to us it seemed quite jungly, with jungly plants growing on the banks and small, jungly cottages built out over the river at the edges. The second cemetery was a smaller one and the caretaker, who told us he was an Indonesian and had been a prisoner of war with the Dutch and stayed on here ever since, said it had been next to a hospital camp during the building of the railway and actually used as a burial ground then. We couldn't actually see the railway from the cemetery but it's not used at all now and must be falling into disrepair, I don't know if you know it but during the war the Thais sided with the Japs as a matter of expediency and actually declared war on England and America, though the Thai Ambassador to America never handed in the declaration and the Americans never considered themselves at war with the Thais. Some Thai country people did their best to be kind to prisoners of war working on the railway but the riverside people are said to have been most unco-operative.

[Handwritten note to Margaret]

I really can't start on another page to round off the cemetery visit! I've been typing with double-spacing by mistake, which makes the letter look longer than usual.

Many thanks, Margaret and Stuart, for copying out Michael's report. I can't pretend we're not proud of it, but I'm sure Ian's and Carolyn's and Nessa's must be as good.

You must be making frantic preparations for your holiday now, and I do hope everything will go well and the weather be good and that the children enjoy themselves and keep fit. Many thanks for treating Michael's ear-ache, by the way. As far as I know, he hasn't had one for a long time, and it was sensible for him to save it up till he came to you! Incidentally, we have a card to say he was due for a polio innoculation in St. Albans last Spring, but of course it's too late now. Do you think it's worth having him done later on? Don't answer this question now. Wait till after your holiday! And don't forget to let us know when you've run out of money.

Did you get him to the dentist all right?

Much love to you all, Averin

26th August:
"A Little Mild Bargaining"

British Embassy,
Bangkok
Thailand.

August 26th, 1957

Dear Everybody,

The day after we arrived here (about June 2nd) Cookie took me out into the back garden and showed me a very sad array of dilapidated objects - two rusty buckets with holes in them, two rusty watering cans with holes in them, a rusty old oven, a shopping basket with a handle missing, a gardener's broom with only about two bristles and an old gardener's basket (the local substitute for a wheelbarrow) which looked very tatty. Cookie's comment on all these things was "Must have new." I sent him off to buy a new oven straight away, and he came back with a large, shiny one with a handsome glass front. Cooking here is mostly done with charcoal and at one end of the kitchen there's a large, formidable stone affair with four round holes in the top, and when you want to boil a kettle quickly you fan the charcoal from on top, and presently tongues of fire come shooting out, and then you put your kettle on. The oven also sits on top of one of the holes, and it has a sort of tray on top on which you put more hot charcoal, and that's the way the Sunday joint gets cooked. I should think Cookie must get pretty cooked too, with all that heat, and I'm glad I don't have to do it.

I didn't do anything about the other dilapidated objects until this week, but now I've learned my Thai numbers and can say "How much is that?" and "That's much too expensive" so I decided I was ready to do a spot of bargaining. My first port of call was a basket shop, one in a whole row of basket shops, each one stacked to the roof with every kind of basket imaginable - little hand baskets with lids (used instead of handbags), marketing baskets, dainty ladies' shopping baskets, laundry baskets, gardening baskets, babies' cradles, basket-work fans, bread baskets, wine-bottle baskets, hampers, trays and dozens more basket-work things which I can't think of. After a little mild bargaining I bought a cook's basket for 20 ticals (6s. 8d.) and then for the gardener's basket I was led through to a shed at the back, where there was one almighty jumble of baskets, and there I bought quite a large one for only 6 ticals (2s.). At the back of this shed the family dinner was spread out on the floor and the children were already squatting beside it, waiting to begin. There was a small but succulent-looking chicken and a bowl of rice and various other dishes, and the chicken and the rice and the other things each had a burning joss-stick stuck into them so there was a great smell of incense. I thought this was very touching and prayerful, but somebody told me afterwards that the Thais use burning joss-stocks to keep the flies off their food! However, the incense didn't seem to affect the mosquitoes which swarmed out of the baskets and up through the floor-boards and had a good dinner off my legs. I stood on one foot and scratched that leg with the other foot, and then I stood on the other foot and gave the other leg a scratch, and as soon as I'd paid for my baskets I beat a very hasty retreat!

Next I went to the tin and aluminium shops where men were busy hammering metal into shape or squatting on the floor, welding with hot irons heated with charcoal. There were stacks of big buckets and middle-sized buckets and little buckets, tubs for washing clothes (or yourself), watering cans and ovens. I got two buckets for 30 ticals instead of the 32 which the man first wanted. Not much of a bargain, but since he'd seen me roll up in our handsome A 95 he obviously thought he'd be foolish to come down any lower. I expect a Thai would have got those same two buckets for about half the price. That was the end of that shopping session for me (this being the rainy season I decided the gardener could wait a little longer for his watering-cans) and I went home and distributed my wares like a princess distributing largesse among the poor, and cookie and the wash-amah and the gardener all expressed suitable gratitude for these things which they were to use on my behalf.

On Saturday evening we went to have a drink with an American friend called Lloyd Burlingham. We met him in Songkhla and he's working for USIS (pronounced YOUSIS) which means United States Information Service and whose object is to tell the Thais all about the American way of life and try to influence them to follow these ways. We have a British equivalent called B.I.S. (British Information Service) but as far as I know it only functions in Bangkok whereas USIS has several branches throughout the country. Lloyd is a great one for psychology and on the wall of his sitting room he had a most extraordinary painting of a face. It was done in oils dabbed on in many different colours and it was quite impossible to tell whether it was a man's or a woman's face, because although it looked like a man's it had sort of black pill-box hat perched on top and there were two ribbon-like things hanging down on either side.

Lloyd told us he had painted the picture that morning and he was very pleased with it. He knew nothing whatever about painting and when he started the picture he didn't know what it was going to be. Gradually a face emerged, and this face obviously belonged to a very unhappy person because it was lined and pinched and miserable-looking. It took him a long time to get the lower half of the face right, and in the end he took a cloth to wipe it out and start again, and as he was doing this he had the distinct feeling that he was actually taking a face-cloth to a real person's face! He couldn't explain the hat, but thought it might represent great mental stress, and when Geoffrey said (jokingly) that the sort of pile of black ribbon on one shoulder looked like a sinister hand, Lloyd was frightfully pleased.

He then suggested that I should take up painting in a similar way. I said I couldn't paint, but he said neither could he -

artistically. The whole idea was to express your inner self in daubs of paint. I said I thought my inner self was all right but he said that was impossible. I was an interesting person, and all interesting people have inner conflicts which need expressing in paint.

(So next time you go shopping, all you miserable, interesting people - Mummy, Dai, Florence, Margaret and Stuart, and all the children too - buy yourselves some oils and brushes and canvasses and express your poor unhappy inner selves!)

After all this I should say that Lloyd is a pleasant, highly intelligent person of about 40 and his party was a great success. As he's not a diplomat it was very informal. Instead of dainty morsels pierced with tooth-picks to eat we were invited to go and put our own slices of ham on hunks of bread, and if we wanted a drink we had to fetch it ourselves. There were Thais and Americans there apart from ourselves and we really enjoyed it very much.

September 1st is (I think) Florence's birthday, so many happy returns, Florence. I wish I'd told the children sooner, but if this letter arrives before the 1st I'm sure they'll be thinking of you and wishing you many happy returns too.

[Handwritten note to Margaret and Stuart]

When Stuart's letter arrived I said, "But Stuart doesn't write letters," and Geoff said soothingly, "I expect Michael's got some small thing wrong with him and Stuart's writing to explain it." We opened the letter with trembling fingers, and lo and behold! Stuart <u>had</u> written a nordinary letter, and we enjoyed it enormously, partly because it was all about Michael and your children (nobody has given me any news about the latter) but also because it was written in Stuart's usual way of talking and I could just see and hear him talking about Michael arriving looking remarkably clean (with a look of astonishment on Stuart's face) and the Stephens attacking the cricket ball with a horizontal bat and all the rest of it. Thank you very much, Stuart, but I'm sorry you felt you <u>had</u> to write. I know how busy you are, whereas I keep a whole morning

91

free for letter-writing every week.

    You seem to have given Michael a wonderful time, and I can't tell you how grateful we are. I nearly squeezed out tears of happiness when you said about him being loveable and obedient and helpful, and all the cricket and everything. I can imagine him saying reproachfully, "But Uncle Stuart, you <u>promised</u> you would," when Uncle Stuart hadn't promised anything of the sort. Sometimes his imagination tricks him into hearing the strangest promises which grown-ups have never made.

    I knew he'd need three more pairs of shoes. But what about house shoes and slippers? He's had the whole lot for a year. He says some boys wear sandals for house shoes, which must be a lot more comfortable, and ordinary Marks and Spencers bedroom slippers. Sorry to trouble you about this, but I don't want his feet squashed, specially in those hard house-slippers.

    Much love to you all, Averin.

P.S. Thanks for taking him to the dentist. According to my dentist's views on diet, all his excellent teeth should have rotted away long ago.

NOTES
Lloyd Burlingham was director of public information for the Southeast Asia Treaty Organization in Bangkok from 1961 to 1965.

2nd September:
"Mr. Dick Whittington"

British Embassy,
Bangkok
Thailand.

September 2nd, 1957

Dear Everybody,

Last Thursday His Excellency the Ambassador, Mr. Dick Whittington arrived in Bangkok, complete with his wife and her cat. They came on a small Danish ship from Singapore and all heads of sections from the Embassy were asked to go and greet him. So at 8.45 a.m. the Hintons set forth in their car and arrived at the docks just as the ship was covering the last 100 yards to the quayside. There was quite a gathering of people there, various Thais, one or two British business men and their wives, the Indian Ambassador and his daughter, and so on. We all stood craning up at the ship, and then at last we were allowed to surge on board and went up to the deck where we were introduced to H.E. and his wife and then invited to tuck in to a feast of caviare and other savouries and champagne. Having only just finished breakfast it was rather difficult to do justice to this remarkable repast!

I must say that first impressions of H.E. and his wife were quite favourable. He had just that small amount of dignity and pomp necessary in an ambassador, and she moved about among us, clutching a bouquet of flowers, in a very amiable fashion. She has greyish but very attractive hair and light blue eyes and, as Geoffrey said afterwards, an ever so slightly common accent, which as far as I'm concerned is all to the good, as I feel that a person with an ever so slightly common background will be far easier to get along with than a member of the blue-blooded aristocracy would be. I suppose she's somewhere in her middle to late forties and he something over fifty, but that's only my guess.

That same evening all the embassy staff, from the Counsellor down to the Thai door-boy gathered together in the Counsellor's house. We were divided up into groups, Commercial section, service attachés, chancery, admin., secretaries and clerks, and presently Dick Whittington and his wife arrived and were solemnly taken round and introduced to all of us. So far we have been living a fairly irresponsible life as far as the Embassy is concerned but we have already felt the grip of the person at the helm. The Embassy wives are all summoned to coffee at the Residency on Thursday and Geoffrey has just rung up to say that he and I must stand by for dinner to-night, complete with black tie and I just <u>hope</u> that doesn't mean a long dress for me. I must confess I find this a little trying because we've done a fair amount of dutiful entertaining ourselves in the last few days and I think we could both do with an early night.

As I told Ann in my last letter we have a Scotland Yard Special Branch policeman roaming round these parts just now.

Sightseeing with group including Geoffrey and policeman from Singapore

He's come out to Singapore to take over from the British

Police Adviser while the latter goes home on leave and the two of them are visiting police officials in Bangkok and Cambodia and Laos and Vietnam. The Scotland Yard chap stayed with us for a few days last week and yesterday he came back for another two nights and we'll have him for one more night next week before he goes back to Singapore. The other man is staying at a hotel but we have to give him the odd meal, and yesterday was a thoroughly disorganised day. We didn't have lunch till 3 o'clock because their plane was late, and then for some reason we didn't have dinner until nearly 9.30 p.m.! I am far too regular in my habits to appreciate or derive pleasure from such happenings. On a Sunday too!

On Saturday there was another official passing through from London to somewhere or other, and he too stayed at a hotel, but we gave him lunch and in the evening we arranged a dinner-party for him and took the party to a night-club afterwards. He was a friend of Geoffrey's and a pleasant chap, and indeed the Scotland Yard chap is pleasant and homely, but when all these things come on top of each other it's a little exhausting.

Last Tuesday (the 27th), when the Scotland Yard man and his friend were here on their first visit, we gave a buffet dinner to introduce the former to various Thai police (the latter has lived in Bangkok, speaks Thai and knows all the Thai police already). We invited 20 police brigadiers, colonels and what-not (note that the Thai police have army ranks) and their wives, and I got into quite a tizzy finding enough cutlery and crockery and glasses, arranging with Cookie about the food, hiring an assistant cook and so forth. Geoffrey got hold of two men servants from the Embassy to come and help and on the appointed evening I spun around, arranging what small tables I could muster around the room, and dotting chairs (10 of which were hired) here and there so that in the end our large sitting-room looked rather like the lounge of a hotel. In the end only 16 police and about 8 wives turned up, so the party wasn't as large as it might have been, which made things easier at the time, but, oh, dear! how tired we got of eating up remains during the next few days! We were warned beforehand that only about half the people we invited would come, but as accepting invitations is not a Thai custom (about a dozen did get round to accepting or refusing) we had to cater for the possible maximum. Everybody who came spoke English, including the wives, and we really had quite a pleasant evening. I suppose we ate at about 9 o'clock, and immediately afterwards the senior Thai and his wife rose to go, and after a discreet pause the Brigadiers departed, and so it went on until we were left to gossip with a few colonels until about 11 o'clock. Thais as a whole are not keen on very late nights because they get up so early in the morning.

I've been having a fairly slack time with my teaching recently because two of my pupils have left for England and the University students and the Social Workers have been having a holiday. But now I'm building up my private pupils again and the holidays are nearly at an end, and I'm wondering how these private activities will fit in with Mrs. Whittington's plans. Will she ask me to accompany her out calling, or to visit hospitals, or to sit on charitable committees? I hope not, but time alone will show .....

NOTES

H.E. is short for "His Excellency" and was the Embassy staff's usual way of referring to the British Ambassador. Sir Richard Whittington was ambassador to Thailand from 1957 to 1961.

9th September:
"Geoffrey was in a great tizzy"

British Embassy,
Bangkok.

September 9th, 1957

Dear Everybody,

It has rained a very great deal during the last few days and everything is damp and sticky. Geoffrey's shoes are covered in green fungus and the books are all going mouldy and the keys of the typewriter feel clammy and even this paper I'm writing on feels limp and moist. When I try to strike a match the outside of the box is so damp that nothing happens. Outside in the garden the grass is sodden and the flower-beds which are humped up like little hills have moats round them which never drain away. There's a family of ducks next door which come in regularly to bathe in our flowerbeds, and the frogs, of course, think it's wonderful. They sing about it at night time and their noise is deafening. We had a man in to dinner last night, a colonel (English) attached to SEATO. He speaks very quickly and in a staccato way typical of English colonels ("Went to a party last night. Absolute heaven. Everybody who matters there. Plenty to drink. Afterwards to a night club. Frightfully expensive. Didn't have to pay.") and because of the frogs and rain neither Geoffrey nor I could hear one word he said. It was all right until he asked a question and then we were well and truly bogged down.

The headquarters of SEATO (SOUTH EAST ASIAN TREATY ORGANISATION) are in Bangkok and this week we had two invitations connected with it. The first said, 'The Minister of Foreign Affairs requests the honour of the company of Monsieur G. Hinton and Madame at a Reception in honour of His Excellency Nai Pote Sarasin, Secretary-General of SEATO on

Wednesday, the 4th September B.E. (Buddhist Era) 2500 at Saranrom Palace from 18.00 to 20.00 hours. Ordinary Dress.' Nai Pote Sarasin, who has been the Thai Ambassador in Washington, has just been elected the Secretary-General of SEATO and this party was given because of that. The Palace was originally built by King Mongkut (and here let me say that in the last letter I wrote about that gentleman I got my historical details all mixed up. King Mongkut is the King of Anna and the King of Siam and Chulalongkhorn was his son. I got it the other way round) and I was all for poking around to find some token of his past glory, but the Saranrom Palace is now the Ministry of Foreign Affairs and all the palace rooms are offices. There were a great many Thai officials lining the hall and the stairway up to the reception room and as we went in we shook hands with all of them. Afterwards I learned that one of them had been Nai Pote Sarasin and one of them the Thai Minister of Foreign Affairs but I regret to say that at the time of hand-shaking I was unaware of the honour I was receiving.

The second invitation said that 'The President of the Council of Ministers requests the pleasure of the company of Monsieur and Madame G. Hinton at a Reception on the occasion of the SEATO Day at Government Residence on Sunday the 8th September, B.E. 2500 from 18.00 to 20.00 hours. Ordinary Dress.' The Reception room here was large and beautifully decorated, with pastel blue walls and the squiggles on the ceiling painted gold. There was also air-conditioning so it was an enjoyable and comfortable party. The prime minister was at the door to greet us, but before we got to him there was a Thai man who murmured discreetly "The Prime Minister is on your left", just to make sure you didn't shake hands with the quite insignificant person on your right. In actual fact the Prime Minister is an outstanding and dignified person whose picture often appears in the newspapers so one couldn't possibly have passed him over, but it was useful to be guided for a newcomer, I'm sure. The whole of the diplomatic corps was there, together with eminent Thai officials and members of SEATO. The men wore their best suits and the ladies a varied assortment of cocktail dresses. No stockings, of course, but one lady wore a hat and you can be quite certain that she was French. At about 6.45 we were each given a glass of champagne and all turned towards one end of the room where the Prime Minister delivered a speech in English and proposed the toast of the King of Thailand and of SEATO whose third birthday it was. Unfortunately I was on the edge of the crowd of people and as we turned towards the P.M. I was in the front row. I tried to edge backwards and mingle with other people but everybody else was trying to do the same and I found a solid wall behind me. While the speech was being made bright lights were turned on us and the ciné cameras whirred. I tried to hold my tummy in and smile and look interested in the Prime Minister's speech but don't much like the idea of appearing in the newsreels at Thai cinemas.

There was a little more speechifying and then the curtains on the stage behind the Prime Minister were drawn back and we were entertained with a performance of Thai classical dancing. This is something which every Thai girl learns in the same way as our girls learn ballet dancing. It has a technique all of its own. For instance, your fingers have to be very supple and you must be able to bend them backwards and move them about separately in this position in various gestures which probably have great significance. You must also be able to hop about on one foot with the other foot up behind, not pointed elegantly in our ballet manner but bent forwards from the ankle in a way which would make Margot Fonteyn's hair turn grey. Performances of Thai dancing can go on for hours and be very tedious but this show only lasted about half an hour and it ended up with a very jolly number with both men and girls, dressed in gay costumes, romping round, the men beating on peculiar drums and a row of men at the back hitting sticks together or striking gongs in time to the music.

This has been a week of great occasions because on Friday our ambassador went to the palace to present his credentials to the King. He took with him his counsellor, his service attachés and his first secretaries, so on Thursday Geoffrey was in a great tizzy gathering all his diplomatic uniform together. He had inherited two separate sets from departed diplomats, together with a box full of brass buttons and clips, a white helmet with a brass spike on top, a sword with a gold tassel hanging from the pommel, and a pair of black boots one size too small. Having chosen the suit (white drill with a high collar on which were clipped two dark blue bands each with two gold stripes signifying his rank of first secretary) which fitted him best he gave this to the wash amah to press while Som See and her mother squatted on the pantry floor polishing the buttons and brass spike and sword and smearing the helmet with blanco.

Geoffrey in uniform for the Ambassador's presentation to the King

Then he borrowed a pair of boots from a third secretary and a pair of white gloves from the same source, and by Friday morning he was all complete. He had two sheets of typewritten paper telling him what he must do, and he went round all Thursday and early Friday morning muttering to himself, "Six paces forwards. Bow. Shake hands. Six paces back. Bow again. 9 paces back. Bow. Turn round sharply. Withdraw," and he really looked quite worried. At ten o'clock on Friday he went to the residence, where the Ambassador and others met together, and then they proceeded in convoy, complete with police escort and in specially provided cars, to the palace. They all carried their helmets and gloves and left them in an ante-room at the palace so the ceremony wasn't as complicated as it might have been, but I gather that some of the partakers got their paces a bit jumbled up. However, these things never matter, and the ceremony was soon over, and back at the residence they all relaxed over a glass of champagne. Their wives miraculously appeared at this point (me among them, though Geoffrey was shamed by my putting in a late appearance) and we all drank champagne together.

Embassy male staff on the Palace steps on presentation of the new ambassador, Dick Whittington, to the King

Naturally H.E. and Mrs. Whittington have been much discussed among ourselves and they seem to have made a good impression. Mrs. Whittington is particularly charming and friendly and we wives enjoyed a coffee morning on Thursday when she asked us advice about dressmakers and hairdressers and discussed charities which we were in the habit of supporting. She's going to have a coffee morning once a month to which we can all go, but only if we want to, and if we want advice at any other time we're to be <u>sure</u> to drop in and ask her!

The dinner party G. and I were summoned to last Monday turned out to be for Sir Donald Macgilliveray, the retiring High Commissioner of Malaya, and his wife. They had arrived from Singapore that morning by air and spent the afternoon sight-seeing in Bangkok and were staying at the residence for a couple of days.

Geoffrey had been told to wear a black tie and cummerbund but as he didn't have a cummerbund he wore a sharkskin jacket instead, and, frankly, I thought he looked very much nicer. We arrived punctually at eight, and presently Sir D. and Lady M. came downstairs, he looking astonishingly young and she a lot older, though as the evening went on you could see that they were really about the same age. They were obviously both exhausted with packing up and farewells and travelling and sight-seeing. Sir D.'s eyes kept on shutting sleepily even before dinner, and Lady M. looked positively grey with fatigue. There were only the six of us and it was the quickest dinner party I've ever been to. 10 minutes were allowed for martinis and we were in the dining-room by half-past eight. (Incidentally, in spite of three electric fans we were kept cool during dinner by a punkah which is a sort of cloth canopy over the table with a chord attached to one end. The chord disappears through a hole in the wall and is pulled backwards and forward by an invisible man.) After dinner we had coffee and liqueurs and then H.E. said, "Well, I'm sure you must be wanting to go to bed," and Lady M. said, "Yes, we are," and up she got and out she went and after a little more polite and lingering conversation the Hintons took their cue and were out too. We were home long before ten, whereas the usual time for a dinner party to end is about 11 o'clock!

It's time for me to withdraw from this letter, too, I feel, or you'll be sick of it!

Averin

G'S ACCOUNT OF THE PALACE CEREMONY.

The do at the Palace wasn't as bad as A. makes out. After a lot of kerfuffle beforehand making sure that one's uniform was suitably clean and pressed, and that the button pins held, it was, I admit, something of a relief, on arriving at the residence, to find (a) that H.E. had got his gorgets on upside down and (b) that one of my colleagues wasn't in uniform at all, but in tails and topper. On a tactful enquiry being put to him, he remarked that as he had never succeeded in getting a uniform allowance out of the Office he didn't see why he should buy a uniform! On which light-hearted note we took off from the Residence for the Palace — the Thai for which is Phraborommabarajawang — the Ambassador and Counsellor in a bright yellow Buick preceded by a scarlet Armstrong-Siddeley with two policemen in it to blast the way, the First Secretaries — seven including me — in two more scarlet A.S., and finally the three Service Attachés with masses of gold braid and gongs, and swords dangling from every hip, in the A.A.'s car. (The Second and Third Secretaries weren't in on this). Two police motorcyclists - on motor cycles - swerved about on either side of H.E.'s car, pushing the traffic into the side, and traffic-lights and level-crossing gates just beginning to fall were treated with like disdain. So we were swept right across Bangkok in some twenty minutes and into the Phraborommabarajawang. Here in the courtyard was drawn up a guard of honour, in uniforms obviously copied from that of a Field Marshal in the Grenadier Guards of the '80s — scarlet tunic and plumed hat. Much handshaking, by palace officials as we went up the steps and into an ante-room, where we deposited our helmets and gloves, were given a soft drink each, engaged in polite conversation and awaited His Majesty's pleasure. Then just after eleven we were marshalled — by the Grand Marshal! (I felt rather like a 10-ton open wagon being shunted very gently but authoritatively by the Flying Scotsman) — into the Throne Hall. We went in twos, I being one of the last pair with one more colleague behind. On either side of the door was a guard in ancient Siamese dress, helmet with side-pieces, baggy trousers and spear. Then came the nine paces, six paces business, after which H.E. moved forward and pronounced a few sentences in Thai before getting down to his speech proper which was in English. The King replied in Thai, and then H.E. advanced, shook hands, and engaged in conversation in (to me at the back of the line) inaudible tones. He then presented each of us in turn, calling out our names, each advanced to within hand-shaking distance of H.M., bowed, shook hands, and returned <u>backwards</u> to his place.

The Throne Hall itself was not very large, but most impressive, especially the lighting. I can't describe it, butperhaps you can imagine something like a cross between an Oxford College chapel and a cave of stalagmites - or better still, stalactites. More marching backwards, this time, in column, with the Chief of Protocol acting as the shunting engine at the opposite end of the train to the Grand Marshal, and we were out in the ante-room again, writing our names in the book, and being given a glass of champagne to toast our Queen and their King. Then another cavalcade back to the Embassy, with more champagne, this time on H.E., and some photographs on the steps of the Residence. And so home to lunch, to put away sword and uniform until December (King's Birthday Garden Party) and return boots and gloves to their owner. Quite a jolly morning, really, and next time it'll be as easy as falling off a log!

With much love to all of you, *Geoff*

[Handwritten note from Averin to Margaret]

PERSONAL

My dear Margaret,

The V.P. arrived about a fortnight ago. The poor thing was very squashed and had burst its bonds, but fortunately you'd wrapped it up well so nothing had happened to smear the secret documents in the F.O. bag! Otherwise I feel there might have been Comments and Questions, which would have caused the Hintons to blush.On the whole Geoff and I have decided we'd better stick to old Ramses, whom we feel we may as well include in our cost-of-living allowance as far as price goes! I'm sorry about this, after putting you to all that trouble, and having prematurely introduced Ian to some of the mysterious facts about birth control. But to have Volpar Paste all over the diplomatic bag really would be rather embarrassing. Anyway, finances are generally a bit easier out here, so to hell with ten bob's worth of contraception! I must just mention shoes once more. You say nothing about football boots, yet I can't believe Michael's are still big enough. And have you remembered the number 24 to be put underneath all the shoes?

Hope the holiday went well.

Love to all, Averin

NOTES

Ian was Margaret's son, my cousin, 12 years old when this letter was written.

16th September: "Getting a dress made to one's liking"

British Embassy,
Bangkok.

September 16th, 1957

Dear Everybody,

My very small number of party dresses have been making such frequent appearances recently that I decided it was time to get some new ones. Nobody ever buys dresses ready-made here, so off I went to Sampeng, the district where there must be at least 100 material shops, and a friend introduced me to an Indian shop, where after much humming and hahing and holding of material against myself I chose a length of dusky pink cotton with a sheen that gives it a silky look (the silky sheen is a good tip for out here because cotton is easy to wash and silk isn't, yet it's nice to have a material that looks like silk!). Then followed a little bargaining with the proprietor about the price and at last he painfully agreed to knock a few (far too few for my liking) ticals off his original sum, so then he cut my length of material and I carried it off to a dressmaker recommended by the same friend.

The dressmaker is a Thai lady with quite an establishment. She has a long hut where her assistants work but her clients go into her private house, first taking their shoes off at the door in the traditional Thai manner. She sat me down with a whole pile of fashion magazines and asked me to find a model which I liked, but I found it very difficult to picture any of those concoctions on myself; besides, I knew exactly what I wanted. I could see my dress in my mind. So I described this dress to the dressmaker - the V-neck and the full skirt - and she said she could make that perfectly. So she measured me (always a distressing business with my large proportions) and told me to come back in a week's time.

When the week had passed I went back in some excitement and tried my dress on, but alas, it was not the dress I had pictured in my imagination. Yes, it had a V-neck, but it was a wide V, not the narrow V I had conceived, and the neckline at the back was lower than I had intended. Instead of looking chic it made me look distinctly blousey. The dressmaker evidently thought so too because she suggested improvements and I'm now waiting to see how improving they are when I go for my next fitting.

All this, of course, is a lesson in the technique of getting a dress made to one's liking. Other people, and especially Thais, have wonderful dresses made for them, but they have been brought up in the art of dealing with dressmakers whereas I am used to buying my dresses off the peg. There were some very luscious dresses, for example, at a dinner party at the Ministry of Foreign Affairs to which we were invited on Thursday this week. Our host was the acting minister of Foreign Affairs (the Minister of Foreign Affairs, Prince Wan Waithayakorn, is busy reproving Russia about Hungary on behalf of the United Nations at the moment) and he had invited us to dineat 8 p.m. The occasion was a sort of final launching for our Ambassador, and the guests were all those members of the Embassy who had been with him to the Palace when he presented his credentials to the king, with their wives. Our instructions from the Embassy were that H.E. and Mrs. Whittington would arrive punctually at 8.5 p.m. and we were to be sure to get ourselves there well before that; so 7.50 saw the Hintons and one or two others cruising gently round the block (which happened to be the Palace) and at 7.55 we all converged on the Ministry of Foreign Affairs and our cars disgorged us at the foot of the carpeted stairs.

As we went up the stairs we were each handed a plan of the table with an X to mark the spot where we were to sit, and then, at the top, there was the usual number of officials who must be shaken by the hand. Finally we ladies were handed on to an inner room where various Thai wives, clad in those gorgeous dress I was talking about, were waiting to receive us. We were all in long dinner-dresses, but the Thais never wear full-length ones, their argument being that it's silly to trail the hem of your dress in the mud and arrive looking grubby. Instead they wore three-quarter length dresses, and I must say they looked just as good as ours.

We sat about on plush-covered chairs for a bit, and then H.E. and Mrs. W. came in, and he was fielded by the men in the outer room while she was passed on to the ladies, and there we sat and sipped cocktails and nibbled niblets until at last the doors at the end of our room were flung open and we were invited in to dine. For a moment all was a-flutter while we found our seats, but at last we had settled down and the meal began. Geoffrey, poor man, was in the angle between two tables, with one of his colleagues on his right, and a Thai lady on his left but behind him, so he couldn't possibly talk to her.

Averin's sketch of seating plan

Opposite him was a most charming-looking Thai lady, but he couldn't speak to her either because the table was wide and it would have been indecorous to shout across. I was more fortunate with a first secretary from our Embassy on my left and a Thai who had been a first secretary in London for five years on my right. He spoke fluent English and revealed that he has left his nine-year old son in England as a chorister at Exeter Cathedral choir school. I find this rather odd as the father is almost certainly a Buddhist, and although Thais have no qualms about sending their children to Christian schools, I shouldn't have thought Exeter school would have accepted a Buddhist as a chorister. Doubtless they expect to convert him!

The dinner — Potage aux haricots blancs, Pinces de crabes à la Mayonnaise, Oie (goose, I suppose, though it tasted like chicken) rôtie à la Vosgienne, Pommes Allumettes, Asperges d'Argenteuil à la Crème, Currie de Boeuf à la Musulmane aux condiments variés, Bombe glacée Alsacienne with Friandises au Chocolat, and, finally, Fruits, commonly known among English-speaking people as pineapple — passed off calmly, apart from a waiter pouring soup (fortunately tepid) in a gentle stream from the tureen down H.E.'s left arm, and ended up with toasts and speeches. I won't say that conversation wasn't a strain, because at times it was, and there were moments when one looked down the table and saw both Thais and English sitting with strained expressions on their faces, obviously wondering what on earth to say next. But there was a Western orchestra supplied by the Department of Fine Arts which jollied us along with familiar tunes, and after dinner, when we moved into the open air for coffee, they played such pieces as Tipperary and Pack up Your Troubles, and it was with great difficulty that I, at least, restrained myself from bursting into song. Mrs. Whittington could be seen beating time and nodding her head, and the Thais looked very happy to see us so happy, and when that particular selection was finished H.E. jumped up and shook the conductor warmly by the hand and then seized the opportunity to say his farewells and depart. It was, after all, eleven o'clock. After a suitable pause the rest of us wound in and out among our hosts, saying good-bye, and then we trailed back down the stairs and out into our waiting cars.

For these sort of occasions Wirart, our driver, takes us, though normally he knocks off at 4.30 p.m. and if we want to go out in the evening Geoffrey drives. But at official functions, when you arrive, you are given a number ticket and your driver is given an identical number ticket, and when you're ready to go you hand your ticket to a man who speaks the number into a microphone and the driver drives up in an approved manner. This is more dignified than parking your car in the road and arriving on foot. Besides, after heavy rain the roads and drives really are very muddy, and even though you may be wearing a short dress, your lady-like shoes suffer horribly. Of course, many people do manage without drivers and nobody thinks any the less of them for it. I think Wirart quite enjoys being in on this sort of thing and he has a good gossip with other drivers while the party is in progress.

Some plane or other must have got held up this week because no mail came in on Saturday and it still hasn't arrived. So I've no letter from any of you to answer, but if they come in sometime to-day I'll add a hasty scribble to each of you.

Much love to you all from us both, *Averin*

[Handwritten note to Margaret]

Letters arrived all right, but nothing more to add. The enclosed photo is rather dull but I thought Stuart might be interested.

Part of War-Graves cemetry at Chungkai

23rd September: "Rudely awakened from his slumbers"

British Embassy, Bangkok. September 23rd, 1957 Dear Everybody, I believe Bangkok actually got into your newspapers this week because of the coup d'état which happened on Monday night. It started off by being quite exciting but now it's petered out and I only remember there's supposed to be a state of emergency on when I see a group of bored-looking soldiers standing at a street corner or a level-crossing or notice the Military Policeman snoozing inside the police hut just outside our Embassy gate.

The political situation had been somewhat doubtful for quite a time. When we came to Thailand the Prime Minister, Pibulsonggram had been in power for donkeys' years but he was pretty unpopular because he didn't do any of the things people thought he ought to be doing. He accepted American money to build a dam to make electricity for the whole of northern Thailand and allowed three super-Constellations to be bought for Thai Airways when people felt he ought to be spending money on improving roads and relieving the lot of the poor. His colleague, General Phao, was pretty unpopular too. He was Minister of the Interior and Chief of the Police, and besides being as corrupt as anybody could be he'd built the police force up into a sort of army, with armoured divisions and paratroops and what-have-you.

Prime Minister Pibulsonggram, General Phao & Field Marshal Sarit

The third big shot in the government, Field Marshal Sarit, seems to have kept his popularity, and it's he who has ousted the other two and set himself up as Military Governor of Bangkok. About a fortnight ago Pibulsonggram was allowed to see that he was no longer wanted. I think 65 members of his party resigned from the government, and at last he was asked to resign. But he wouldn't go. So he was told that if he didn't go the army would be brought in, etc., etc.

At 6.30 on Tuesday morning this week Geoffrey was rudely awakened from his slumbers by the Military Attaché who summoned him to the Embassy. There he found that H.E. had been up since 4 a.m. when a delegation consisting of two Palace officials and two others had arrived to inform him that martial law had been imposed but that British lives would not be endangered and that British property would be protected. Pibulsonggram had disappeared. He was rumoured to be driving north, driving south, driving east, leaving for America in his private yacht, hiding in the British Embassy, in the American Embassy. What a mystery! It was almost exciting. Besides, the roads in Thailand really are bad and one couldn't imagine him driving in any direction for very far.

For several days he was reported to have been seen here, there and everywhere, but now at last he's known to have been given asylum in Cambodia. His brother has been coming to me for English lessons and he seemed to have definite news of Pibulsonggram's escape. His English is really very bad and difficult to understand but it seems that Pibulsonggram was short of money and short of food and wandering about through a forest to get to the Cambodian frontier, which was hardly suitable or dignified for an elderly gentleman like himself. General Phao, on the other hand, was escorted to the airport and put on a plane for Switzerland with two of his closest police minions (and companions in dishonesty). Geoffrey happened to be at the airport when he was crossing the tarmac. There were several tommy-guns about but nobody hustled him and the old rascal was grinning all over his fat face. It seems typical of Thai face-saving courtesy that instead of being dishonoured he's been given the post of adviser to the Thai Legation in Geneva. Field Marshal Sarit, too, keeps declaring his love for Pibulsonggram and saying he wished he hadn't left the country; that if he stayed he would have been treated with all honour and affection (but not as prime minister).

So that's the coup d'état, and things seem to be simmering down now, with a temporary prime minister forming a temporary government. I dare say things will hot up a bit when they hold a general election in three months' time but nobody expects anything so violent as actual fighting. One or two people may be killed by hired political assassins but nothing more than that.

Our other excitement this week has been something quite different. We got an invitation from the head of the British Council, Robert Bruce, to go to a reception in honour of Stephen Spender, the poet, and Angus Wilson, the novelist, who were passing through Bangkok on their way home from a P.E.N. international conference in Tokio. Perhaps I should explain that any V.I.P.s passing through Bangkok are fielded either by the Embassy or the British Council and looked after by them. Navy, Army and Airforce officers (here for SEATO, for example) are conducted on sight-seeing tours by the Naval or Military or Air Attachés or their wives. Journalists and press representatives are dined and fêted by the Information branch of the Embassy. Our most junior third Secretary in the Embassy seems to spend his time going out to the airport at the most ungodly hours to greet and send on their way such Queen's messengers as pass through bearing diplomatic bags. The British Council deals with cultural and intellectual bods, and that was why it was their job to give a reception for Stephen Spender and Angus Wilson, and also, incidentally, to arrange for Stephen Spender to give a lecture at the University.

When we arrived at the party there were already a great many people there and Stephen Spender, a huge, rather bear-like man with grey, wiry hair, a sun-tanned face and blue eyes, clad in

113

a dark blue tropical suit and mopping continually at his far-too-hot face with a handkerchief, was standing there surrounded by a small group of admiring listeners. I was introduced to him (Geoffrey had to go off on the irritating but normal pursuit of trying to field a man from Cambodia whose plane was 2 hours late and had to be greeted suitably at his hotel; but he came back and was introduced later) and asked polite questions about his visit to Japan. I imagine everybody asked the same questions but he was obviously used to this sort of thing and chatted on endlessly and amiably about Tokio and how he would like to stay in Japan for several months and what were his impressions of the conference. I didn't breathe the word 'poetry' because I'm not a poetry fan and haven't (or rather, hadn't) read a single poem by Spender. I have read a few since but as these were all written before 1940 I expect he's forgotten them himself by now.

Having exhausted my questions with Stephen Spender I then passed on to Angus Wilson who was quite a different type of bird. He also has grey, rather wiry hair and blue eyes and was pleasantly sun-tanned, but he's smallish and rather effeminate and when he became excited his voice became quite squeaky. He used to be a librarian at the British Museum but when he was 35 he started writing and he became so successful, especially in America where you get very well paid as a writer, that he gave up his job and now lives on his literary earnings. With him, too, I avoided the subject of his actual writings because I've never read anything by him, but here again, since the party, we've managed to borrow one of his books and both propose reading it.

The party was scheduled to end at 9 p.m. but it was 10 before the last guest departed, except for a chosen few of us who were invited to go on and dine at a Chinese restaurant. We sat round a round table and here the great men shed their jackets and rolled up their sleeves and the thoughtful lady on Stephen Spender's right produced a tube of mosquito-deterrent cream with which he anointed his arms, and everything became far more informal. We ate sharks fins and fried prawns and other delicacies with red chop-sticks and Stephen Spender ate enormously of everything (I think he had five helpings of the last course which consisted of fried rice and pepper-hot soup). And all the time they talked and talked about Japan and intellectual young men in England and finally about India, and at midnight, when they ought by rights to have been worn out by a day of travel and sight-seeing, when we were all drooping with exhaustion and when the restaurant people were obviously dying for us to go, they were still tossing the ball of conversation back and forth from one to the other. Quite obviously this was a professional business with them. They have given so many lectures in so many different countries and been interviewed by so many different people that words flow from them in a endless stream without any effort. However at last, after Robert Bruce had twice said how late it was and the restaurant proprietor had switched the lights out (but hastily put one or two on again), Angus Wilson said he thought they ought to go because they were going for a 7 a.m. trip on the river, and the party broke up.

I'm feeling very irritable because the weather is very hot and sticky and the typewriter is misbehaving and threatening to break down completely at any moment (rusted by the humidity, I fear) and I had indigestion last night and didn't sleep much. If you can't read parts of the letter I apologise. I've done my best under difficult circumstances!

Much love to you all from us both, *Averin*

30th September:
"Like being in a plastic bag"

British Embassy,
Bangkok.

September 30th, 1957

Dear Everybody,

On Monday morning last week an office order, signed R. Whittington, was circulated round the Embassy. It was headed, 'Mourning for King Haakon' and told us that that worthy monarch had died on September 21st and that Court Mourning had been ordered for a fortnight. 'During that period', it said, 'members of the staff should not attend any official function (with one or two specified exceptions). Any private hospitality should be given on a small and informal basis and there is similarly no objection to accepting informal invitations (which involve no special jollification such as dancing or going to the cinema). Dress when appearing in public during the period of mourning should be: Gentlemen: White or dark-coloured suit and black ties. Ladies: Black dress.'

This was rather irritating, especially for the ladies because nobody likes wearing a black dress in a hot climate. I for one didn't have a black dress but I compromised by wearing a black skirt and white blouse when I went to the University or elsewhere to teach, and in the meantime rushed off to buy a length of black cotton and thrust it at my dressmaker who very obligingly made it up into a dress in three days. But even this wasn't very suitable for evening wear and New Zealand had to celebrate its National Day without my assistance. I just stayed at home. The next night we were invited to a cocktail party and I tried wearing a blackish nylon dress which I have, but this is an experiment which I shall NOT repeat. It was like being in a plastic bag with my body getting hotter and hotter and no way for the heat to escape. The men, of course, didn't suffer at all. Their suits are mostly white or off-white anyway, so it was only a question of wearing a different tie.

Geoffrey has now joined a second club, the British Club — the first was the Royal Sports Club of Thailand, if you remember. Long before the war the British Club (which probably had a different name then) had only a very few exclusive members, mostly senior managers and directors of British business firms in Bangkok. When their finances became a bit rocky they invited other, lesser mortals, to join, but those being the days of Class these junior members had to treat their seniors with great deference. Then the war came and the Japanese used the club as an officers' club, but after the war the Thais returned the building to the British and paid up 100% on all damages claims and even went so far as to re-stock the bar with alcohol. Now almost every British person in Bangkok belongs to the club. It has a membership of 1600 and everybody is very jolly together. It's quite a large house with a billiards room and a reading room and a bar downstairs and upstairs two large rooms used for table tennis and dancing. Every Sunday evening at 7.30 they show a British film in one of these upstairs rooms and yesterday we saw 'The Divided Heart' which was on in England before we came away, but we didn't see it then. In the garden of the club there are about 6 grass tennis courts. Very few people are playing tennis just now (I think there are two hard courts at the Sports Club) because of the rain, but very soon now the dry season will begin and then tennis and cricket and racing and so forth will be in full swing.

(When the Thais became allies of the Japs during the war all the British population were interned. The Embassy people were quite comfortable because they were interned in the Embassy compound. I suppose it was rather boring but at least they had plenty of room and a nice big garden. The Whittingtons were here then but after a time they were exchanged for Jap internees in England. The non-Embassy British didn't fare quite so well. They were interned in some other building and got bombed by American planes, which can't have been so jolly.)

To go back to the British Club, most of the members who use it frequently belong to the big export and import trading firms, some of which have been established in Bangkok for a great many years. For instance the Borneo Company, which imports everything from motor cars to ovaltine, is said to have received an order from King Mongkut, a great many years ago, for one English Governess, and that is how Mrs. Leonowens (the Anna in 'Anna and the King of Siam') first came here. So at the British Club one sees quite a different set of faces from those we usually see in the diplomatic round. The traders accuse the diplomats of not using the British Club enough, in fact of being 'snooty', but I think the truth is that diplomats have so much enforced social life that they don't feel the need to go and be merry Britons together in the way that other people do. Furthermore, these business chaps really seem to want to get together and to escape from the Thais, whereas we quite enjoy mixing with people of other nationalities and find Thais very pleasant company.

I don't think I've ever really tried to describe Thai people to you. On the whole they're much shorter than we are, both men and women. I suppose the average height of Thai women is about 5 feet, and some of them are a good few inches shorter than that. They're mostly very slim too and some of them keep their figures after having large numbers of babies, so that you're suddenly astonished to find that a youthful-looking lady is a grandmother. Their skin is dark, but when you've lived here for a bit you forget about that so, again, you get quite a shock when you learn that they feel very strongly about the colour bar question. They have very good and charming manners towards each other and towards foreigners, and a deep feeling of respect for their superiors. When they greet each other they put their hands together in front of their faces and bow their foreheads down to touch the tips of their fingers, but with Westerners they like to be Western and to shake hands. Parents in better-class families are great disciplinarians and girls in particular suffer from this. They aren't allowed out in the evening except under heavy escort. University students suffer in the same way. Those who come from outside Bangkok live in hostels and have a housemother, who has all the authority of an ordinary mother, to look after them. If the girls want to go out in the evening they have to do battle with her, while the men usually get permission quite easily.

Right at the bottom of the social scale you have a very different picture because the children are not only undisciplined but often unwanted and from a very early age they roam around on their own and sleep anywhere out of doors and keep themselves alive by begging and thieving and gambling. This sounds almost impossible but it was a probation officer who told me that children of 7 have been convicted of gambling. Up to the age of 18 these young people who are caught are either sent to approved schools or put in the care of a probation officer, but after that the only punishment is imprisonment. Of course there are hundreds of poor Thais who bring their children up well, but this small core of young criminals must be quite a problem to somebody.

The political situation here has calmed down now and although there are still a few soldiers and sandbags and guns about I think they'll gradually disappear. Pibulsonggram is now trying to get back into Thailand to settle his affairs but it doesn't look as if he's going to be allowed to come. His brother hasn't been to me for his last three English lessons and he hasn't sent any message so I don't quite know what's happened to him. Perhaps he's lost his job as director-general of the Ministry of Transport, or perhaps he's busy trying to help his brother. My chief interest in his movements is financial because this is the last day of the month and he owes me nearly seven pounds and if he never comes again perhaps he'll never pay me!

Much love to you all from us both, *Averin*

[Handwritten note to Margaret]

Surely we must owe you some money by now? How much was Michael's school bill?

NOTES

The King who died on 21st September was Haakon VII of Norway.

7th October:
"Life is not so rosy this week"

British Embassy,
Bangkok.

October 7th, 1957

Dear Everybody,

We had a terrific storm a couple of nights ago. It thundered and lightninged and a great gale blew and at least one bushy tree in our garden was blown down and broken irrevocably at the stem. The rain simply pelted down and next morning it was still pelting and the whole garden looked like a lake. Lots of people had gone to bed in the usual manner with all their windows open, and woke up to find themselves and their beds and their rooms saturated. That all started 36 hours ago and it's still raining, though not so hard, and of course everything inside the house is damp and sticky, and there's the problem of how to get the washing dry, so in some ways life is not so rosy this week.

However, it is a bit cooler, and this morning I even put on my cardigan because I felt a bit chilly. Towards the end of this month the rainy season is supposed to end and the 'cold' season begins. At its best this season is said to be very pleasant for Europeans, with a nip of sorts in the air in the morning and evening, and a nice dry, Mediterranean heat during the day. In Bangkok the temperature doesn't go below 50°F but in the North of Thailand it can be really cold and poor people who haven't adequate clothes suffer and even die.

We've had a very busy week with people coming and going. Geoff had to attend a SEATO conference at the beginning of the week and he had two official cocktail parties and one dinner party connected with that (he had to drive home from the latter in the middle of the thunder storm, which wasn't very funny). Then there was a man out from London who had to be shepherded here and there and entertained for five days. He and we were invited to lunch at the residence on Friday. We had it very informally at a small table in a sort of wide passage between the dining-room and the garden. It sounds rather draughty to you in England but in Bangkok there just aren't any draughts. Life might be pleasantly cooler if there were. Mrs. Whittington asked Geoffrey if he was related with some Hinton or other of whom we've never heard. There seem to have been several Hintons roaming round the Far East in recent years and we're always being asked if we're related to them. One bachelor was even congratulated on getting his wife out here at last but his name was really Lynton and his wife was me! After lunch, when the men were chatting together over coffee Mrs. Whittington discussed gardens and gardening with me — a topic which didn't please me at all as gardening is not my strongest subject of conversation. However, I managed to make suitable encouraging noises and she burbled with the satisfied egotism of the real gardener.

Early in the week an official (a friend of ours and also a woman) stayed the night on her way through from Phnom Penh to Singapore and at the end of the week we organised a supper party round the man from London and took the whole lot on to a piano recital given by a French pianist called Lilamand, organised by l'Alliance Française in Thailand.

Into the midst of activity (rather confusing to you because I haven't given anyone a name, but I don't think names would help you much) came a man from St. Albans called Sander. He wrote to us about three months ago and said that he was an orchid grower going on a world tour and that Mr. Hessler suggested he should look us up. He asked if he might spend one night with us and one with a Thai acquaintance and we said we would be delighted, but in the end he didn't stay with us at all because the Thai was very affronted with the idea of sharing his guest. The Thai put him up at the Erawan hotel, which is a very new and posh and modern hotel with air-conditioning in every bedroom and a garden-courtyard in the middle with a kidney-shaped swimming pool filled with very blue water in it. The arrangement was that we should meet the man Sander at some point during his stay, but as the time grew nearer I grew more and more worried as we seemed thoroughly booked up with all these official engagements and there wasn't a single meal left (except breakfast) that we could invite him to. However, he got booked up too, and in the end we met beside the Erawan swimming pool at 11 o'clock at night, after the piano recital! By this time Geoffrey was very weary and sat with his eyes half closed all the time, but the man Sander really <u>was</u> an egotist (Mrs. Whittington, of course, isn't one; I merely made that remark to cover up my feeling of inferiority over gardening) and talked about his own affairs and himself through two rounds of drinks. He told us about his tour and his nursery in St. Albans and his wife and his five children and how his visitors always go in at the back door, and how he loathed the socialists, and how miserably socialist the present conservative government is. He told us how his grandfather's home had been what is now the conservative club in St. Albans and his grandfather's nursery a vast province which took in the whole of Clarence Park. I think he was a little astonished that we had obviously never heard of him, but he was so busy passing on to his next point that that was soon forgotten. We never really fathomed the purpose of his tour, because it was assumed that we already knew all about it, but we gleaned that he is a member of the Royal Horticultural Society and I think he'd been to some world conference and was very pleased because he'd snubbed the Australians and fixed that next year's conference should be held in London.

He's an odd-looking man, rather small, with grey, tightly curled hair, very sun-burned, and speaking in a deep, educated voice. I say this because from the writing and style of his letters we'd quite expected a Secondary-Modern type with a Hertfordshire accent, so that was quite a shock to <u>us.</u> Just as we were saying Good-bye we managed to slip in the information that we had three children in England, and then he was all agog to do anything he could for them, like popping into the Army and Navy Stores and buying them little presents, but as this sounded rather expensive we declined the offer. Perhaps I should now counteract some of my cattiness by saying that he really was quite a pleasant and interesting person, but I do like conversation to be two-sided. He'd been spending his evening giving a lantern talk to a group of Thais so perhaps he just hadn't managed to shake off the non-stop-lecture manner.

One night we went to dinner with some American friends, a youngish married couple with more money than most, I think. They have a most delightful house with shiny wooden floors and modern upholstered furniture (most people have bamboo cane furniture with fitted cushions on the chairs) and lots of pottery and ornaments and nick-nacks picked up all over the world. They have a whole library of long-playing records and throughout the evening there was a background of classical music. The invitation specified sports shirts, and the Americans all wore these coloured, loose shirts which hang outside the trousers, but the British arrived rather self-consciously in long-sleeved white shirts with ties but immediately took the ties off and undid the top button. We had dinner at a very long table (there were 24 of us) on the verandah, and because it was the host's birthday, we had for the sweet birthday cake and ice-cream. The cake was covered with icing and candles (too many to count, but the birthday man blew them all out in one breath) and its inside was plain sponge with a cream filling. Just like one of our own children's birthdays, in fact, especially when we all started singing 'Happy Birthday to You.' One of the British said afterwards how childish it all was, but I rather enjoyed it and I don't think it does any harm to be childish once in a while.

It's afternoon now and still raining. I've discovered that when the match-box gets too damp to strike a match on you can dry it out by holding it against a lighted electric light bulb. How's that for ingenuity?

Much love to you all, *Averin*

[Handwritten note to Margaret]

Many thanks for your letter and for all clothes-mending etc. on Michael's behalf.

Cheque enclosed (I hope!)

No, on second thoughts, not. G. has to pay out large sums for children's holidays this week, so if it's orl right by you, and as you've £5 in hand, he'll send you a cheque nearer the Xmas holidays. I've made a reminding note in my diary.

14th October:
"A philosophy, not a religion"

British Embassy,
Bangkok.

October 14th, 1957

Dear Everybody,

There was so much flooding at the beginning of this week that Suk, the gardener, caught a fish on the back lawn, and it was big enough for him to cook it and eat it and give some to Som See. Where did the fish come from? All right, I'll tell you. There's a khlong (canal) at the end of the garden and our floods are just an overflow from that. Actually, to look at it you wouldn't know it was a khlong at all because it's so thick with water plants and weeds, you can't see the water. There's another smaller khlong at the side of the house which has overflowed into our garden too, and although the floods are subsiding now the two-foot high posts on which the house stands have still got their feet in water.

More flood news: Geoffrey arrived at the Embassy one day to find that the concrete apron in front of Chancery was all awash, and the only way to get from the car into the building was via an upturned wooden packing case (but not a very large one) which had been put there as a stepping stone to the higher, drier steps. Anyone calling at Chancery, even those in the higher ambassadorial ranks, had to enter by this precarious route, but what happened to anyone who arrived on foot I can't imagine. On the same day I went to the university to take a class and found the same sort of conditions prevailing, except that there was no packing case, and because of cars parked in front of the entrance I couldn't get anywhere near the steps. Daroon, the administrative man who is my help and stay in the university was standing at the top of the steps and called out that I had better wait until the tide went out. This wasn't a joke. He seemed to think that the floods really would be affected by the fall of the tide, though <u>which</u> tide he meant I'm sure I don't know, because the river is a long way from the university. However, I decided that even if this did happen it wouldn't be until long after my lecture hour was over, so I took off my shoes and paddled, and the students who had been standing on the upstairs verandah, waiting to see how the English woman would deal with the problem, gave a great shout of appreciative laughter. During my lecture I told them I'd bring a swim suit next time, and they thought this was very funny. One of the ways of telling how much they can understand me is by telling a joke. If they laugh I know I'm making headway, but if there's a loud silence and polite, solemn faces, I know my vocabulary's got too difficult for them.

However, it doesn't look as if I'll need my swim suit, because after days of depressing, continuous rain, the sun came out at last on Saturday and things are beginning to dry out a bit now.

On Thursday we gave a dinner party to nine people, a Thai lecturer in engineering at the university and his wife, a government social welfare worker who has been a good friend of mine ever since I helped her to write her speeches for the Asian women's conference (His name is Luen and hers is Warunee and their surname is Bintasan, but when introducing them you call them Mr. Luen and Mrs. Warunee. It's the Thai custom not to use the surname, which makes it very difficult sometimes for Westerners to fit husbands and wives together at a party. The Americans, who prefer to impose their customs on others rather than try to adapt themselves to their surroundings stick firmly to the Mr. and Mrs. Bintasam business but the British struggle on with trying to do things the Thai way. The Thais, being naturally polite people, are worried by the confusion, and the wife of one of their foreign office officials told me that protocol department is trying to evolve some ruling in the matter), our Thai teacher, Khun Suphat (Khun means Miss, Mrs. or Mr. and Suphat is her first name), Mr. and

Mrs. Skiff (he's a second secretary at the American Embassy), Mr. Gilmour (parson of our church) and his wife, and Alan Leavett (first secretary, British Embassy) and <u>his</u> wife. It must sound to you as if we live somewhat extravagantly with all these dinner parties and things, but the fact is that entertainment of Thais and non-British diplomats and non-diplomatic British is one of our duties and we get financial allowances for doing it. If you invite a few embassy friends in for a drink or to dinner you can't put in for the allowance, but if you include some of those other bods you can, so naturally you do, mostly. Of course, we do sometimes just invite friends.

With a largish number of guests the usual thing is to have a buffet dinner, and when there are Thai guests you get your cook to make a Thai curry with rice and a European dish, so that there's something for everybody. Everything is very informal and people sit about with their plates on their knees and the servants flit around gathering up the empties and seeing that people's glasses are filled with whatever they want to drink.

On Thursday evening the Thai guests left at about 11 o'clock (they get up at 6 a.m. or earlier so they never like to stay out late) and when they had gone I produced a pamphlet on the progress that has been made on the understanding between Anglican and Presbyterian churches which Mummy had sent me and which had arrived that morning. I gave it to Mr. Gilmour (a Scots Episcopalian) and he was glad to borrow it, though he said he'd read parts of it in the Church Times, and then, one way and another, we got talking about religion and Christianity in Thailand and Buddhism, and it was very interesting. Mr. Gilmour's theory is that although a few educated Thais are Buddhists in the accepted sense, the majority of Thais are really Spiritists, which means that superstition plays a large part in their lives and they spend a lot of time trying to placate whatever spirits happen to be roving around. If they place a burning joss-stick in front of the image of Buddha in a temple it's only because they feel he's a person who might do them harm if they don't ingratiate themselves with him.

Spirit house in the garden at 46 Soi Lang Suan

It's generally accepted that Buddhism is a philosophy and not a religion. In other words, it recognises no God (all living things have natural origins) but recognises a sort of spiritual unity in the whole universe. And the true Buddhist is tolerant towards Christianity because the Christian outlook is just part of the natural order of things. But the lesser-educated Thais, who are really spiritists (and this includes some so-called Buddhist priests who have great influence with the people) are intolerant towards Christianity, with a result that Thais who become Christians sometimes have a hard time. If a member of their family has bad luck or is ill, the Christian is blamed because his 'god' is the evil spirit. Mr. Gilmour told us about a young Christian mother who committed suicide because the priests and her family persecuted her with a persistent form of black magic; and when Thais come to him and say they want to become Christians he often feels very anxious, knowing what troubles may lie ahead for them, especially as they may go off to their villages where there is no Christian community and nobody to give them moral support. It sounds rather like what one reads about darkest Africa, and I suppose it's the sort of thing that happens in any under-educated, superstitious community. I don't think that school children are taught much about Buddhism in schools. Every young man is supposed to do a minimum three months novitiate in the priesthood but apparently the girls are left to get along as best they can, so probably spiritism flourishes in their minds.

This is only another aspect of Buddhism and what Mr. Gilmour said. For myself, I haven't really found out any more about it, and Alan Leavett said afterwards and he would have liked to take Mr. Gilmour up on several points. So don't accept it as the whole truth, although of course Mr. G.'s personal experiences must be true.

Some time ago our noisy Thai neighbours left the house next door and for about a month a whole army of servants scrubbed and cleaned and painted it and pulled down a rotten pergola which acted as a screen between us and them and tidied up the garden, all under the supervision of the very charming-looking landlady who strolled about in jeans or sometimes just sat down and watched. Often operations went on into the night with the aid of a searchlight. Quite a lot of people came to see over the house (I believe it was unbelievably dirty) and one couple seemed to come several times, and in the end they came with all their luggage and settled in. They brought two small children who seemed remarkably quiet and well behaved after all the noisiness and wailing of the Thais. They were Americans (Mrs. Curiosity Hinton could distinguish their voices easily from a distance of thirty yards) and the other day I decided it was high time I called on them, so round I went, having first noted through the very sparse greenery which now divides the two gardens that Madame was sitting on the verandah. It's an enormous, three-storeyed house built mostly of wood, but the downstairs consists mostly of verandah. The sitting-room and dining-room are on the first floor, with a wide balcony all round the outside of them, and on the top floor there are just two enormous bedrooms and a bathroom. I didn't see any of this but Mrs. Wilcox told me about it. I found her to be a lady with a nose with an almost right-angled hook in it, and Cathy, the 7-year old daughter, who greeted me with "Hi! Do you have any children?" had the same Semitic appearance, but Pop and Junior (alias 6-year old Robbie) looked like average Americans, with close-cropped hair. They were all very friendly and Pop introduced himself as a Doctor of Philosophy here on a one-year's contract to teach Public Administration at one of the Bangkok universities. There are a lot of American professors and lecturers here on this contract business. It's part of the American aid plan, and at the same time a lot of Thai professional men go to the States to increase their learning on a scholarship basis. Put crudely, of course, it's part of the American scheme to impose Western culture upon the Thai way of thinking and to counteract Communism, but there's no doubt that the Thais benefit by it because their own education standards are so low.

I have now played my third game of bridge and am beginning to have some glimmering of understanding about the mysteries of bidding. I even know what a grand slam is and such expressions as 'length rather than strength', 'singleton' and 'finesse' are beginning to have vague meanings attached to them. We went to the house of the Military Attaché, Colonel Potter, and his wife (they live just over the way) who invited us on the understanding that we were learners rather than players, and they gave us such sympathetic treatment that I think we both learnt a lot. The game was preceded by an excellent dinner of soup bespattered with fried breadcrumbs, roast pigeon, buttered boiled potatoes, crisp potatoes and French beans, followed by ice cream and jam sauce, so altogether it was a very pleasant evening.

Did I speak too soon about the floods subsiding? Here comes the rain again, but let's hope it's only a shower.

Much love to you all, *Averin*

[Handwritten note to Margaret]

MARGARET, PERSONAL

Dearest M.,

Grandpa thinks Michael needs a new suit so I've told him to go ahead and buy one. I expect his present ones are getting a bit short in arms and legs, and Auntie Gran is very particular about appearances. Will you see he wears out the discarded suit in the

131

holidays?

I wish you'd come to do some marriage guidance here. Our driver's wife is just about to have her fourth baby, & I swear the oldest child isn't 6 yet.

Much love, Averin

P.S. One of my English pupils, a Thai woman, tells me she's been sterilised. This apparently is legally permissible if you've had 4 children, but too expensive for the driver's wife, I fear!

NOTES

Averin's sister Margaret was a qualified doctor and now working part-time as a Marriage Guidance Counsellor.

21st October:
"A most frustrating country"

British Embassy,
Bangkok.

October 21st, 1957

Dear Everybody,

This is assuredly a most frustrating and irritating country in a great many ways, although it's good fun in others. For instance, I was taking a class at the British Council the other day and one of the pupils said she wanted to come to me for private English lessons. I said I was very busy but she insisted, so in the end I agreed that she could come for her first lesson at 8 o'clock this morning. So up I get, bright and early, and have my breakfast, and by 8 o'clock I am ready for her; but does she arrive? No. She comes (with many apologies) at twenty past eight, but of course I can't give her an hour's lesson because I have another pupil at nine o'clock. Actually for her to come at all was quite remarkable. It's not unheard of for a student simply not to turn up, or to ring up when the lesson's due to begin and say he's not coming. The number of hours I've wasted just sitting at home waiting for people must be quite considerable.

And then again, there's the matter of the septic tanks. Several months ago, owing to a persistent and ever-increasing smell, we learned that there is no main drainage in Bangkok but that we have a septic tank which has to be cleared out regularly about once a year, and that the septic tank for the bathroom is UNDERNEATH the verandah. So a little man came along and picked a hole in the verandah tiles, and then, in the dead of night (they always function at night), the municipal pumpers came and pumped, and next day the little man came and put the tiles, back, and charged something under six pounds for his services. It then gradually dawned on me that there must be other septic tanks in the compound and indeed I learned from Cookie that there are five in all, one for each of our bathrooms and one for each servants' house. All right, so they must be pumped out. But in the meantime one servants' house must have a new W.C., and the builder comes along and puts it in and cements the floor beautifully, but when I talk about the septic tank I learn that it is under the cemented floor and that we must pay to have it broken up and then re-cemented after the pumping has been done. This is enough to drive anybody mad. But what about our downstairs bathroom? The septic tank is immediately underneath the beautiful white-tiled floor which must be hacked to pieces before operation pumping can be set in motion. The municipal pumpers come again, but Cookie has not yet contacted his floor-hacker, so they go away again. They come again (at 3 a.m.) but this time they say that the job must wait until the floods have subsided. And so it goes on. Frustration and irritation enough to send you up the wall.

To turn to a more savoury topic, yesterday was the Harvest Festival at our church and the building had been draped and decorated in the usual manner by the ladies of the parish. The flowers in vases looked very nice, but alas, the creeper and greenery that had been hung over the pulpit and electric lights and the usual pieces of furniture had withered away in the heat and looked very sad. There were one or two marrows and bunches of bananas and bags of rice but most of the gifts consisted of tinned foods, because fresh fruit and vegetables perish so quickly in the heat. There were a great many children there, including brownies, clad in sleeveless light brown, thin cotton dresses and no hats, and cubs in thin khaki open-necked, short-sleeved shirts and shorts, and at the beginning of the service they all processed up to the altar with their tinned gifts. After that we ploughed the fields and scattered in the usual manner, but I must confess I did miss the smell of a Harvest Festival in England. Geoff says it's the apples that smell so good.

On Thursday morning this week, after lecturing at the

university from 9 to 10 I went along to the Sports Club and played badminton with two Australian friends. They hadn't the first idea how to play and I had rather forgotten, but it was good fun; and afterwards, when we were good and hot, we all had a swim in the swimming pool. No, Florence, we didn't catch cold. Don't forget that the water would be nearly 80°F., and with the sun shining brightly you just couldn't feel anything but pleasantly cool and refreshed. The idea is that we should make a regular Thursday morning do out of this, but unfortunately (in this respect) I've agreed to take on a job at the British Council from the beginning of November, so I shan't be able to go many more times.

About a fortnight ago, Robert Bruce of the British Council asked me if I would be his P.A. (personal assistant) and I was terribly flattered because nobody has ever <u>asked</u> me to do anything before. Geoffrey asked H.E. if it would be all right, and H.E. said he thought I ought only to do it part time because as an embassy wife I mustn't get so tired that I can't fulfil my social duties satisfactorily. So I shall go mornings only, but I'll still be doing a bit of teaching in the afternoons and evenings so it's all rather silly. Still, I rather enjoy the teaching and wouldn't like to give it up altogether.

For a long time Geoff has been needing a pair of light-weight black evening trousers, so on Saturday evening we visited a series of tailors and discussed prices with them. The first, a Chinese, wanted 550 baht (57 to the pound) but came down to 500 when we said it was too much. The second, also Chinese, said he would do it for 450 bahd and the third wanted the same amount, but his material was rather inferior. The fourth, a Saigon tailor, wanted 400, so Geoffrey stuck to him. The trousers are to be fitted to-day and ready to-morrow (Tuesday), in time for a black tie dinner with the Portuguese Chargé d'Affaires. I hardly think Austin Reed could be relied on to complete such an operation in three days!

Much love from *Averin*

27th October: "A procession of cars slithering about"

British Embassy,
Bangkok.

October 27th, 1957

Dear Everybody,

Sunday afternoon, and a very hot one too. It's been oppressively hot for the last few days, although the rainy season hasn't come to an end yet and we've had one or two heavy showers. The garden's still flooded too and a sort of pontoon has been built by the steps to take the place of the upturned packing case. This flooding is quite unusual and the most widely-held explanation seems to be that, with a lot of new buildings going up, khlongs have been unscientifically filled in and there's nowhere for the water to drain away to.

Although it's so hot a sort of autumn seems to be in progress. One or two trees have some really lovely reddy-brown leaves on them, and the creeper over our verandah has some not-so-lovely yellow ones. Spring seems to be in the air too, though. Birds are flitting about in pairs (some of them in and out of the house) and singing and twittering and calling to each other in a purposeful manner. Altogether I think the only conclusion one can come to is that things don't happen here the same way as they do in England.

Geoffrey is asleep upstairs with the air-conditioning on.

Last Wednesday was Chulalongkhorn Day and a national holiday, so we had a holiday too. We decided we'd go to the seaside and we invited two friends (Arthur Maddox, 1st Secretary, SEATO) and Pat Barnes, an Embassy girl secretary (note the small s) to go with us. We started at about 9.30 and after about two hours' driving we came to Bang Saen, where there's a perfectly good beach, but for some reason we decided to go to Patia, where Arthur and Pat said the beach was much better, and it was only about an hour's drive on. Almost immediately the road deteriorated. It was full of sudden dips and bumps, thanks to the rains and floods, and at one point the metal surface had been washed right away and there was about 20 feet of mud churned up by buses and cars. However, the mud was fairly firm and we managed to crawl through without damaging the car unduly. After what seemed ages we came to the turning off to Patia. It was an unmetalled road, and here again, in a dip, there was a bad patch where part of it had been washed away, but we managed to get by safely.

It was nearly one o'clock when we reached the beach, but we decided to have a swim first before eating, and the water was beautifully warm and calm and fairly clear. When we felt hungry we came out and I got the lunch things while Pat retreated to the car to dress, and then it started to pour with rain so we all made a dash for cover. Geoffrey and I got in the car in our swimsuits but Arthur said he was going to stay outside, since he was wet already, so we handed his sandwiches out to him (it was at this point that I discovered Cookie had only packed sandwiches for two instead of four; my fault, I think, for not telling him) and I'm sure they must have been sodden with rain before he got them into his mouth. It simply pelted with rain and by the end of half-an-hour a beer-glass which we'd left on the grass outside had more than an inch of rain-water in it. However, it stopped eventually and we all got dressed, and, since we were uneasy about the road, we started off home again. Trouble started at the first flooded dip. From a long way off we could see a crowd of Thai country folk gathered round a car, and a man coming our way told us we mustn't go on. However, we saw the car leaving the dip behind it all right so we pressed on, and the crowd waited to see what would happen. We all got out to inspect and found that another big chunk of road had been washed away, and the mud that was left was soft and sodden, but Geoffrey decided to have a try, so he drove slowly on, and the next thing was that the back wheels were spinning merrily round, mud was flying in all directions, and the car was sliding gently sideways towards the fallen-away edge. Being true-blue British (also, Arthur had guests at 7 p.m. so we had to get home) we remained undefeated, and we three went behind and pushed, and when the Thais saw we meant business they pushed too, and at last, with great squelching and sucking noises the car heaved itself out onto the firm road again. Arthur, Pat and I were covered with wet mud from the waist downwards but we didn't care. It was all rather fun. I had a tin of 50 cigarettes in the car and we gave this to the Thais, who gave a great cheer and then swarmed round the poor man who was holding the tin. Geoffrey was afraid he'd be left with it, but with no cigarettes for himself, but I hope he managed all right.

The 'main' road by now had several streamlets rushing across it but all was well until we got back to the first bad patch, where there were about six buses queuing up on either side, and a solemn procession of cars churning and slithering about, with anxious passengers pushing and heaving while the drivers sweated and accelerated and tried to steer through the least damaging way. We tacked on and Pat and Arthur and I received a little more mud, but in the end that obstacle was passed too and we were able to press on home without more serious difficulties. We stopped off at Bangsaen for a quick snack (fried prawns for some, bacon and egg for others) at 4 o'clock, and then raced back to deposit Arthur at his house at 6.20 - just time for a quick shower and change.

That evening there was a big United Nations party to which we were invited. It was given in the Santitham Hall which is a large air-conditioned place with head-phones attached to each chair, for international congresses. We arrived late and sat up in the gallery at the back, so the first performance of Thai classical dancing looked very colourful but we couldn't distinguish very much of what was going on. It was followed by a so-called 'Musical Play' about the United Nations Charter and given by the children of the International School. The International School is run mainly for Americans by Americans and it has a reputation for a low standard of education and unruly discipline, but children of other nationalities do use it for lack of anything better, and I thought that it was undiplomatic to say the least of it that all the children who took part were Americans. However, it was a terrible play - awful fourth-form stuff - and I would have burned with shame if any child of mine had been in it. Fortunately the last item on the programme was a performance given by first-class Chinese tumblers and conjurors, so it ended on a happy note. After that we swarmed into an adjacent hall were the men fought for refreshments and then we all danced. There were people of almost every nationality you can think of there, and quite a lot of them were wearing their national costumes. There were Thais, Japanese, Russians, Philipinos, Vietnamese, British, Americans, French, Indians, Pakistanis - dozens more, I expect, although I didn't identify them.

We were pretty weary so we left soon after twelve. When we got home Wirart was out in the garden, bare to the waist and wearing a local garment whose name I haven't discovered - a short piece of material wrapped round the waist, up through the legs and tucked in at the back. He was luring fish with a stick which was burning at one end, picking them out of the water and popping them into an empty petrol tin. One way of getting your family's breakfast!

Last time I wrote Geoffrey's new black evening trousers were in the hands of the Saigon tailor. They were, in fact ready in three days and on Tuesday evening he picked them up at 6 o'clock, and at 8 o'clock he was wearing them at the Portuguese Legation, where the Portuguese Chargé d'Affaires, Senhor Santos-Matias and his wife, were giving a dinner party. I suppose there were about thirty guests and it was quite a gorgeous affair, with the men in white sharkskin jackets and black ties and the ladies in long dresses. Again, it was an international do, with German, Thai, French, Japanese, American, Pakistani and British guests, and after having warm soup served to us in cups, we all went and helped ourselves to food in the dining-room and took it back to small tables where we sat and ate. The Portuguese Legation is an old building with enormous rooms, so the drawing-room (on the first floor) is very suitable for such a party, but Senhor and Madame S-M's bedroom is almost the same size and seemed very barely furnished. There were two single beds in it, each tucked away in a corner with about 20 feet between them, two dressing-tables, a wardrobe, a couple of chairs, and that was all. Fifteen ladies powdering their noses after dinner took up about as much space in it as fifteen peas in a large saucepan. The Legation is by the river and there were coloured lights in the garden between the river and the house, so it was rather pleasant looking out of the window (when one wasn't busy engaging or being engaged in conversation). It must have been nearly midnight when the British Military Attaché (ranking as counsellor and the most senior person there) rose to go and swept his wife out with him, and after that we all said good-night and wended our way home.

On Friday November 1st Geoffrey and I are going to Chiengmai in the North of Thailand by train. There's a British Consulate there and Geoffrey will be taking the diplomatic bag. The journey takes about 20 hours so we'll spend one night on the train and then about three nights in Chiengmai before we come back. I don't quite know how we'll manage next week's letters to you all but I dare say we'll keep in touch somehow!

Much love from *Averin*

[Handwritten note to Margaret]

Many thanks for your long letter of the 20th. Geoff is going to try to remember to send a cheque with this and I hope it'll arrive in time to pay for the new suit. Mr. Hinton did have some money for expenses but they never tell us how it's lasting and whether they need more, although we keep on asking. I didn't realise he had sent you a bill for Michael's expenses. Under the circumstances I think you'd better pay for the suit.

I've told Mummy not to bother about everyone sending

Christmas presents, but I'm going to try to find out about bag regulations.

I certainly mixed the Marriage Guidance Council up with the F.P.A. but now know better!

Love to all, A.

NOTES

Mr Hinton in this case refers to Geoffrey's father Dai.

31st October:
"Make your mouths water"

British Embassy,
Bangkok.

October 31st, 1957

Dear Everybody,

As it's only four days since I last wrote I haven't really got any news so I'll make this a foody letter. I'll make your mouths water with fresh pineapples and succulent cuts of roast pork and beef and dishes of the very best fried Thai rice. All these things are local and therefore comparatively cheap. You see herds of cows in the country and they are used for beef only because Thais never drink fresh milk. This sounds extraordinary, but perhaps it's just as well because lots of people would know nothing about sterilising milk and in the hot climate lots of germy things would go wrong with them. When Thai babies are weaned they go straight on to solid foods with rice as the staple diet, and though you might expect rickets and bad teeth to ensue the majority of Thai babies look remarkably sturdy and grown-ups have white, even, strong-looking teeth. Thai pork is supposed to be among the best in the world. When a pig goes to market he's pushed into an openwork basket which just fits his poor tubby little body and sometimes you see several of these things in a lorry, with just a row of curly tails sticking out of the ends of the baskets. Pigs in pokes, in other words.

We buy a good deal of our food from the Embassy 'Commissary' where prices are a good deal cheaper than in the shops. It's run as a side-line by a Second Secretary in the Embassy and I think he buys most of the things from Singapore or Hong Kong. We can get Australian and Danish butter there (Australian 4s. 8d a lb, Danish 5s. 4d), margerine, cooking fat, tins of fruit and vegetables, jams, honey (3s. 10d a lb jar), cereals, legs of lamb, pheasants, hair-shampoo, tins of tea, coffee and biscuits, and tinned milk! Just to give you an example, a 1 lb jar of honey in the town costs 9s. 6d and a lb of Danish butter 8s. 4d. No wonder business people who don't have access to the Commissary complain of the high cost of living! We can also get duty free wines and spirits and cigarettes from the Commissary . The shop-keeper is a little Thai man who sits at a table and tots up your bill when you've helped yourself to whatever you want, and he's helped by an even lesser individual who climbs up the shelves when you can't reach something (he wears no shoes) and then carries your goods out to your car.

In spite of all this Cookie sets off for market every morning at about half-past six and buys all the fresh food, like eggs and meat and vegetables and rice. We don't have potatoes very often because they're very expensive. He also gets bread, which is baked by the Little Home Bakery and always tastes very nice and home-like. Goodness knows where Cookie goes to market or what he does when he gets there because he rarely comes home before 10.30, and when he does come he drives up in great state in a samlore, for which he charges 2 ticals (8d) a day. Som See's mother gets our breakfast every morning so all Cookie has to do is to cook lunch and dinner, and possibly cut a sandwich or two for tea if we feel hungry. This is quite normal procedure for a cook in Bangkok, just as it's normal for Som See and her Mum to clean downstairs from 7 till 8 a.m., cook and wash up breakfast and make the beds and then disappear for a couple of hours to get their own breakfast and relax. After that there follows a little desultory cleaning upstairs, followed by the laying of the lunch table and the serving of lunch, but after that there's another restful lull until 4 p.m. when one of them comes in to tidy up and empty ash trays and so forth. If we have friends in to drinks Som See is pretty busy, and if we have a dinner party they don't get to bed until midnight sometimes, but nobody, however fertile his imagination, could suggest that they, or any Thai servants, are hard-pressed. For their arduous services Som See and her mother get a combined wage of about £11. 10s a month and Cookie a little more.

But to get back to food, there's a very wide range of fruit which grows in Thailand, including those pineapples I spoke of and tangerines and bananas and a sort of cross between a grapefruit and an orange called a pommelo. When we came here we tried all sorts of others but they were all either too full of pips or too tasteless or too sickly-sweet so we don't get them any more. What I'm really waiting for is the mango season. I'm not sure when that begins, but it must be about February or March, because somebody told us that another name for the hot season, which starts in February, is the Mango Blossom Season.

And now for a complete change of subject just to finish up with: one day last week I went to have my hair washed and set and at the same time had a manicure and pedicure. This is a very fashionable occupation and the pedicure is more popular than in England because most ladies wear open-toed shoes (or no shoes at all inside the house). To have your hair washed you always lie down on your back on a sort of plinth with your hair hanging over the basin. While it's being set and dried two Thai girls arrange themselves on stools beside you and one does your finger nails while the other attacks your toes. But the toe girl doesn't only stick to nails. She gets a bowl of water and scrubs your legs with pummice stone, and when she's done that she scrubs your feet and the SOLES of your feet. Then follows a lot of clipping and filing, and finally four layers of varnish go on to finger nails and toe nails - undercoat, two coats of colour (fingers and toes to match, of course) and one coat of transparent 'fixer'. While all this is in progress it's quite impossible to read a book or magazine, and it takes so long that your hair is just about dry by the time it's finished........

Much love from Averin

P.S. We can receive reasonably sized parcels by bag, but we can't send any!

8th November: "A wonderful three days in Chiengmai"

British Embassy,
Bangkok.

November 8th, 1957

Dear Everybody,

We arrived back from Chiengmai the other day to find a nice pile of letters waiting for us, and four of them told us that there had been no letter from us that week (though Florence, who wrote later than most, said that it turned up eventually four days late). The older generation was quite convinced that I was lying at death's door, but the younger generation tossed it off as a mere inconvenience. Ann remarked philosophically that the letter 'would no doubt come tomorrow' while Michael was 'rather surprised' that it hadn't come (like a tolerant school-master rather surprised that you hadn't managed to give your homework in). Anyway, I'm glad the letters did arrive and I hope last week's efforts behaved better. Florence told us Michael had started Asiatic flu, but he must be better by now. Ann seems to be indulging in all sorts of un-lady-like practices, like going to a birthday party for which 70 crumpets had been ordered, and doing the 'cupboard act, which consists of jumping from the top of the cupboard onto mattresses, pillows, fire blankets and eiderdowns. Did you ever do the cupboard act, Mummy?' No, I certainly did not. From Jill there's a glorious silence, but we've learned that this usually means she's been invited to spend the week-end with a friend - such a frequent occurrence now that Mrs. Tomlinson says that she (Jill) is delighted when Mrs. T says she really must stay at school and write some letters.

In a letter Dr. Graham wrote to us a couple of weeks ago he wondered cynically if 'Asian' flu really started in Asia or whether here it was called 'Western flu' or the 'American ailment', but I can assure him it really started in the East and was called 'Asian flu' even here. When we first arrived in Thailand it was raging just as it's been raging in England and the newspapers were full of it. Schools were shut down and office staffs were depleted and the government was quite worried. The usual percentage of under-nourished and feeble people died, and that of course was NEWS. Quite a lot of Europeans got it (and Americans) but the Hintons were tough after their long sea voyage and didn't succumb.

We had a wonderful three days in Chiengmai, up in the North of Thailand. It's only three hundred and something miles away from Bangkok but the train journey takes nearly nineteen hours to get there. Geoff says this is partly because of the narrow guage, which prevents the train from hurrying through flat country, partly because there are a lot of stops and partly because, as you get nearer Chiengmai, there are a lot of hills to chug through. These hills are a most wonderful experience for anybody who has been living for some time in the flat plain round Bangkok. You wake up at seven in the morning and let down your shutter (which is covered with fine wire mosquito mesh), and there you are, right in the midst of tree-covered hills on a gloriously sunny morning. Don't ask me what the trees are called because I don't know. Some of them are probably teak because Chiengmai is a district where a lot of teak forrestry is done. I only saw one tree of the pine variety during the whole trip. The air was so fresh at that hour of the morning that I felt positively chilly. I had a cardigan at the bottom of my suitcase but I couldn't be bothered to dig down for it so I just sat and hugged myself until it warmed up.

We were met at Chiengmai by the consul's wife, Mrs. Jacobs-Larkcom, who is mentioned in the book 'Journey through Thailand' which Mummy has been reading. Geoffrey was carrying the diplomatic bag (a miserable little canvas bag with very little in it; the only thing which gave it dignity was the metal seal on the string which tied it, and a large label saying ON HER MAJESTY'S SERVICE) so after we had had a quick wash at the hotel we went on to the consulate where the bag was handed over into consular hands and we were given lunch. The consulate is a large white stone building, characteristic of all British government buildings in the Middle and Far East, with a spacious and well-kept garden (tennis and badminton courts, of course), right down by the river which runs through the middle of Chiengmai. Mrs. Jacobs-Larkcom is a Scottish woman with a kind heart, and her husband a quiet bespectacled man of sixty-something who is due for retirement in a couple of months' time.

Our hotel bore the grand name of 'Chiengmai Railway Terminus Hotel', but that was about all that was grand about it. It was a long wooden bungalow building, with a central space for lounge and dining-room, and on each side of that four bedrooms leading off a balcony. The floorboards thoughout were bare and unpolished and the furniture was nothing to write home about, but it was quite adequate. Our beds had high posts sticking up from each end and these supported cotton mosquito nets (as a matter of fact there were very few mosquitoes and I imagine this is because Chiengmai is in a malarial area and a lot of D.D.T. spraying is done by the public authority). At the back of each bedroom there was a bathroom with wash-basin, shower, Shanghai jar and dipper and W.C., where the water flowed freely if a little murkily, though that didn't matter as we were kept supplied with cold boiled water in a large thermos for drinking. In front of each bedroom there was a verandah with cushioned cane chairs and a table and a ceiling fan. The hotel was at one end of the town so it was almost in the country and seemed blissfully peaceful after Bangkok.

But the whole town was much quieter and more countryfied than Bangkok. There were comparatively few private cars and almost everybody, men, women, children, Westerners and all, went about on bicycles. This is quite impossible in Bangkok, where only boys and men use bicycles. There were quite a lot of buses, and one kind in particular annoyed us very much. They were great splashy Japanese-built monsters which snarled like racing cars. Their home-base seemed to be the station square which was just over the road from us, so whenever we were sitting peacefully on our verandah, or clinging on to the last hour of morning slumber the blissful moments were punctuated by their gross growls. Geoffrey and I walked about quite a lot, but when we were too hot or too tired we went in Samlores. These accommodate two Thais very comfortably, but for two Europeans (and one of them fat Averin) things were not so easy and one of us (usually thin Geoffrey) got squeezed forward in a perched and undignified posture. There was one night-time hazard in these samlores, and that was the clouds of insects which milled round the street lights, right down to street-level. If the samlore-driver didn't dodge them you got your hair full of the things and some of them got inside your shirt or blouse and of course couldn't get out. They weren't usually the biting sort of insect, but little green hoppers like minute grasshoppers, but it wasn't very nice feeling them crawling about inside.

For our first whole day in Chiengmai we hired a car with driver at great expense and want up Doi Suthep, which is the highest hill near there, about 2,000 feet high. The road started off with a good surface but rapidly deteriorated so we had to go very slowly. It wound up and up through the trees until at last it came to a tiny village with nothing but atap huts (the roofs and sides made of dried leaves), and there we got out and climbed up 204 steps to a temple called Wat Phra Thart Suthep. This is supposed to be a very holy temple but there wasn't much to look at inside it - just a golden Jeddi and some rather peculiar mythological pictures of incidents in the life of the Buddha, painted in somewhat garish colours. But the view down the hill-side and over the Chiengmai valley was wonderful. When we had 'done' all that we wound our way down again and ate our sandwiches by a whacking great waterfall, and then visited the zoo which was quite nice though small and very hot because it's new and the trees are too young to give adequate shade. We had hired the car for the day and Geoffrey was determined to get his money's worth so we next drove back to Chiengmai and 46 kilometers on in the other direction to an irrigation works which is quite a beauty spot, with a dam and flower gardens planted round it, but we were the only visitors that day. We drank some fizzy lemonade there and strolled around a bit and then drove back to the hotel, but kept the car to go to church at the American Presbyterian Mission Centre, where we sang lots of jolly hymns with a great body of American missionaries and their families and were rather startled when the time for announcements arrived and these were made by members of the congregation. The American Presbyterians seem to be the main missionaries in Thailand. They have a mission hospital in Chiengmai and quite a large centre here in Bangkok, and it was they who started the church of Thailand among Thais and made it an independent body.

The main attraction for the female tourist in Chiengmai is the market where you can buy all sorts of things very cheaply. The stalls are all packed together in one large square, most of them shaded by paper umbrellas, though there's a fish and meat section which must be the most hygienic in the East, with a covered-in roof and glass all round the outside. On the stalls you could buy materials, shoes, trinkets, pottery, straw hats, and all sorts of fruit and vegetables. There are four industries connected with Chiengmai, cotton-weaving, silk-weaving, silver smithing and lacquer work and the products of all these are sold in and near the market. I had a great time doing my Christmas shopping for the children and those most nearly and dearly connected with them in England (all other deserving candidates for gifts will have to wait till we come home) so my next move is to hurry up and get them posted off. I hope to goodness they'll arrive, but with the Thai post being so unreliable nobody knows what may happen. We managed to send Jill's birthday present home with somebody going by plane and she's probably got it by now.

On one afternoon Mrs. Jacobs Larkcom took us in her car to the village where the cotton is woven and we were able to watch the girls at work (it reminded me somewhat of visits to Scotland and the tweed mills). A lot of the materials have what look like elephants and various other things embroidered on them, but they're really woven into the cloth. There is also an umbrella village where all the paper umbrellas are made and waterproofed, and a silver village and a lacquer village, but we didn't get round to seeing any of these.

So that was Chiengmai, and very nice too. When we got back to Bangkok it seemed even hotter and stickier than before, though most of the floods have dried up, and we were out to a dinner party the very first night, and the telephone kept on ringing (mostly wrong numbers) and there were a thousand and one things to see to and to remember and to do, and the house was encased with bamboo scaffolding, with a host of painters painting its outside, and there was a vet's bill of 95 ticals for Doddick who had got himself terribly mangled through fighting over some unworthy bitch. But these are only minor irritations and pleasant things happen too. There was a full eclipse of the full moon last night and to-night we're going to a cocktail party to greet the Marquess of Reading, and this afternoon I'm going to visit a Thai silk factory, and to-morrow night we're going to play bridge (my fifth effort), and on Monday I start work at the British Council so I've said good-bye to my 360 university students .....

Much love to you all, Averin

15th November: "A hive of activity"

British Embassy,
Bangkok.

November 15th, 1957

Dear Everybody,

Our house has been quite a hive of activity during the past ten days. Every morning a team of smart young men arrived at eight o'clock, dressed in clean starched shirts and neatly pressed trousers. They disappeared discreetly round the back for a few minutes and then re-emerged in the dirtiest assortment of stained garments imaginable, leaving their clean clothes suspended from our washing line. These were the painters, and they swarmed in and out of the house, leaving splodges of paint everywhere, over furniture and carpets, drinking innumerable bottlesful of fizzy orange and leaving the empties all over the place, padding about amiably in their bare feet, climbing in and out of windows and generally making themselves at home. In the middle of every morning a rather scruffy-looking man, with a bamboo pole over his shoulder, came jogging up the drive. The pole had some sort of container slung from each end, and in the containers were steaming hot saucepans and enamelled bowls and spoons, and as he came up the drive the scruffy man gave a loud shout, and the painters dropped their brushes and crowded round him and bought their mid-day meal. At five o'clock they put on sarongs and disappeared into the wash-house and at 5.15 they disappeared for the night a respectable group of well-dressed young men (leaving their more disreputable garments scattered round our back premises).

Meanwhile Suk, the gardener, busied himself with thinning out the greenery round the verandah, and then, one glorious day,

Som See misinterpreted a suggestion that all dead leaves on the trellis should be removed and we came home to discover that every stitch of creeper had been torn down. The effect at first was rather startling and naked, but now that the painting is finished, it's rather nice to see the house looking fresh and spruce, with its cream and chocolate brown woodwork (British Railway colours, to Geoffrey's delight) and pale green stone balustrade, instead of the great mass of greenery which shrouded it before. And by the time the hot season comes and we want more protection from the sun, the creeper will have crept up again. By that time too, I suspect the paintwork will be ready to be hidden again. It doesn't seem very good paint. If you touch it by mistake you only have to run it under a tap and it comes off quite easily!

To-day all the scaffolding was taken down and piled on to a lorry, some of the worse splodges of paint were washed off the concrete path at the back, the young men tied their dirty clothes and sarongs up in newspaper, the remaining supplies of paint joined the scaffolding (but Wirart arrived just in the nick of time to remove most of it to paint his own house), the foreman asked if we had any complaints to make, and then, finally, when everyone was satisfied, the team withdrew. There's still the bill to pay, of course, but fortunately this house, like several others, is negotiated by the Embassy and payment for decoration and major repairs is not our responsibility.

Geoffrey has been at home with a feverish cold for two days this week, but he's back at work now. He seemed to be worn out when we came back from Chiengmai, so perhaps the germ was already with him then. I started working at the British Council on Monday (it's Friday afternoon now) and the days seem to have fled by. My exact job doesn't seem to have taken shape yet but I've browsed through quite a lot of files and taken a certain amount of vague action. The office consists of the Representative (Bruce), the Assistant Representative (Evans), and English book-keeper (Mrs. Hack) and me. We all sit in one nicely air-conditioned room together. In the next, not so nicely air-conditioned room there are two Thai ladies who are shorthand typists and a rather more superior Thai lady who is more of an assistant. Then there's a Thai lady librarian in charge of the fair-sized library (fiction, non-fiction and all free) and a Thai lady who guards the newspapers and periodicals in the reading-room downstairs. The two short-hand typists were rather put out by my appearance because they said if I was a secretary too there wouldn't be enough work for them to do but Bruce assured them I wasn't <u>really</u> a secretary. Nevertheless I think I am one so if I have to write a letter off my own bat I type it myself instead of dictating to them, and they find this very bewildering. But so far they've all been very helpful and friendly and nobody gets annoyed if you interrupt to ask questions, and I think I shall enjoy it very much when I've got the hang of things.

One thing I've realised this week is the really acute problem of Bangkok traffic. It's always been very tiresome going out shopping in the morning because everything's so slow moving, but from 8-9 in the morning when everybody's trying to get to school or work by private car, the whole thing just seizes up. I'm sure that if you looked at Bangkok from a helicopter at that time of day you'd see all the roads as one seething mass of stationary or crawling vehicles. To get from here to the British Council on a clear road shouldn't take more than fifteen minutes, but it quite often takes an hour, and when the sun is blazing through the window onto your back it's not at all pleasant just sitting about in traffic jams. The trouble is that there's no really good system of public transport. The comparatively few buses are hot and crowded and the trams are dirty and slow. So everybody who has a car uses it - with disastrous results. Geoffrey's very lucky because his daily trip to work consists of driving to the end of our lane, cutting through the main-road heavy line of traffic (aided by a policeman), and nipping 200 yards up the road to the Embassy. I leave the house at 7.50 a.m. He leaves at 8.40. Theoretically we both start work at 8.30. In practice we probably both start at 8.45.

Averin

16th November: "The most wonderful Christmas of their lives"

[Handwritten letter to Margaret]

Bangkok.
November 16th, 1957

My dear Margaret

Thank you very much for your letter of the 10th. Probably G's father has written to tell you they didn't buy the suit after all. There was no time, and anyway the one Michael was wearing wasn't too bad.

I wonder what Mummy will decide about the Hospital Service Scheme. I told her I thought it looked as if we'd have to join it, but now what you & Stuart say makes me think we were quite wrong. Probably Mummy won't have done anything yet because nothing can happen now till next term.

I'm quite sure the children will have the most wonderful Christmas of their lives, shared with other children. They may have missed us sometimes while we're away, but I often think they live much fuller lives in our absence, and they must gain as well as lose by it. You of course will be frantically busy at Christmas, but spare a thought for G & me without the children! I'm sure we shall feel most peculiar.

Much love to you all, Averin

21st November:
"Great emotional upheavals"

British Embassy,
Thailand.

November 21st, 1957.

Dear Everybody,

Last Sunday morning a friend called David arrived from Singapore with the diplomatic bag. He was staying the night with us so after lunch we asked him to choose whether he'd rather snooze during the afternoon and go out in the evening, or go out in the afternoon and have an early night. In spite of the fact that he hadn't been to bed at all the night before (he'd been to a dance till 4 a.m. and had to catch his plane at 6) he chose to be entertained in the afternoon, so we drove him out to Nakorn Pathom so as to give him an idea of the Thai countryside and show him the Pra Cedi, which is quite something to see. The road was shockingly bad almost the whole way, full of sudden little dips and bumps, and much worse than when we last went along it (to the war cemetries at Kanchanaburi and Chung Kai), thanks to the rains and floods. It must have been quite a strain on the driver (Geoffrey) but David somehow adapted his body to the sudden lurches and leaps and slept soundly for quite a lot of the way. So much for the Thai countryside.

It was dusk when we got home and we were immediately pounced upon by Som See who announced that Wirart's wife was in great pain and must go immediately to the hospital to have a baby and could Wirart borrow the car. We had told him a month ago that he could have it when the need arose so we quickly bundled out and he and his wife and their three children (aged about 4, 3, and 1) and Suk all bundled in and drove off, and half an hour later they all came back minus the wife and told us they had arrived in time. Next morning Wirart asked for six days' leave so that he could look after the children and when we came home for lunch he'd learned by some magic means (probably our telephone) that the baby was a boy. He seems to be a most domesticated father, able to cook and do everything else for himself and the children and there seem to be no signs of distress during mother's absence.

At lunch time to-day Som See, who acts as general interpreter for the whole compound (she's an intelligent child and now speaks English so well that sometimes when she catches me in an idle moment she becomes quite a little chatterbox), announced that Wirart was in financial difficulties over the hospital bill so Geoffrey went and had a man-to-man talk with him and very quickly parted with 200 baht. It's a recognised thing that the employer is responsible for his servants' medical bills. If we go to a European doctor we have to pay enormous fees (mercifully refunded by the National Health Service) but fortunately Thai doctors charge much less for treating their poor patients, even when they know a Western employer is footing the bill. There seems to be some special scheme for hospital treatment too. After all, 200 baht is very little to pay for a confinement.

Apart from Doddick, who is hardly a servant but has produced his share of medical bills, we've had to dispatch Som See to the doctor once or twice, and now Chai, Som See's mother, has embarked on a programme of visits because she's going to have a baby. This is her thirteenth pregnancy, though only four of the twelve previous offspring have survived. She has a very tiresome and undesirable husband who doesn't normally live here but who rolls along occasionally and demands food, lodging and money from her. He frequently gets drunk on rice whisky and seems somewhat mental as even when he's sober he's always holding long conversations with himself. Whenever he comes we have great emotional upheavals and Chai goes around looking very unhappy and sometimes Geoffrey is called in to send the man away. This isn't at all easy as he never wants to go and although

Cookie and all the other servants beg us to call in the police Geoffrey says you can't ask the police to remove a husband just because his wife doesn't like him. Last time he came Geoffrey told him he'd charge him 50 baht a night hotel bill for living on the premises, and oddly enough it had the desired effect and he hasn't been seen for over a week. It's quite a normal practice for the husbands of women servants to live in idleness in the wife's accommodation in the compound so we're really fortunate that Chai's husband has a house elsewhere and only turns up when he's sober enough to remember that he has a wife.

I once asked one of my lady pupils if divorce was a possibility and she said it was a very easy matter if both parties agreed to it. They simply have to go together to the Sheriff and say that they want a divorce and that's all there is to it. But Chai would have to embark on legal proceedings and that would be far too expensive.

One day last week we were invited to dinner at the Hoi Thien Loo which is about the poshest Chinese restaurant in Bangkok. Our hosts were the proprietor of the restaurant and one other Thai and the guests of honour were our ambassador and Mrs. Whittington. Apparently the hosts and the guests of honour had known each other during H.E.'s more carefree days in Bangkok some years ago. H.E. was asked to bring along so many British guests, so he invited all the First Secretaries and their wives, and the Counsellor, and also Sir Robb Scott, Commissioner General for S.E. Asia from Singapore, and Lady Scott, who happened to be in Bangkok, with their daughter and son-in-law who are with them on a visit from England. There were quite a lot of Thais there as well, including Prince Prem who was educated in England, Eton, I think, and Oxford, and has a most astonishingly Oxford manner and speech. Some of the Thai men were wearing suits made of Thai silk which is woven for men's wear to look like a sort of flecked tweed.

The dinner-party was held in a very tastefully decorated

private room in the restaurant and when the time came for us to eat we sat round three round tables with about ten people at each. There were the usual Chinesey courses served from a bowl in the middle of the table into an assortment of little China bowls which were set before us and we ate with ivory chopsticks, though little china spoons were provided for the more sloppy courses. The whole evening was livened by a Thai band which played tinkly, waily classical music (I mean Thai classical music) throughout the whole three hours we were there. The members of a Thai band sit shoeless on the floor and play instruments which could be classed as percussion, wind and strings, though none of them resemble Western instruments. Every now and then a woman singer made her contribution in an extraordinary harsh voice. To do this properly you have to be a professional with strongly developed throat muscles as all the sounds are produced from the throat rather than from breath expelled freely from the lungs in the way we sing. I can't really describe the technicalities, but because of the way they are trained Thai singers find it very difficult, or even impossible to sing Western opera or lyrical songs.

To go back to Thai silk, I thoroughly enjoyed my visit to the Thai silk factory some time ago. We saw raw silk, and boiled, clean raw silk, and dyed silk, and silk being spun and silk being threaded on the looms and silk being woven by hand. Some of the materials were too gorgeous for words, with one coloured thread woven across another to give a most luscious effect. Some of them were woven with silver and gold untarnishable thread. When we had seen everything we were each given a silk stole and handbag to match, each costing at least four pounds in the shops. Mine are blue woven with silver and with pink spots embroidered on them. Thai silk is quite expensive to buy in the shops here, but at Liberty's in London I believe it costs about 12 pounds a yard! If your Christmas presents arrive safely some of you will receive less expensive examples of it.

On Saturday Geoffrey and I have been invited by an ex-pupil of mine to spend a night in her bungalow at Bangsaen, by the sea.

I have to write my letters to you at the end of the week instead of on Mondays now so I'll be telling you all about this visit when I next write.

Much love from Averin

29th November:
"Week-end by the sea"

British Embassy,
Bangkok.

November 29th, 1957.

Dear Everybody,

Since I last wrote the nicest thing that has happened to us has been the week-end by the sea. Our hosts were a Thai lady called Chirapa and her husband (whose name I didn't discover), a forestry expert at Siraja, working in the employment of the crown. I used to give Chirapa English lessons and I first met <u>her</u> through Mrs. Warunee, the Social Welfare expert, who you may or may not remember from a previous letter. Anyway, Mrs. Warunee and her husband, Mr. Luen, were guests for the week-end too and we drove them down in our car.

During her first lesson Chirapa seemed rather a timid little person, in fact she burst into tears at one point because she was telling me her life history and her father, who was English (also a forestry expert) was burned alive when their house caught fire, when she was three. She wanted to know about English etiquette because they have to entertain German visitors (the common language being English) and she wanted to know how to tell them lunch, or dinner, was ready, and what to say when it was time to leave the table. After the first lesson she blossomed out and grew quite friendly, and our invitation to the seaside was the result.

Sirija is a large village, or small town, right by the sea, and Chirapa and her husband have a house at Bang Pra, a small collection of houses a couple of miles away. They live in Bangkok during the week because the husband has to do office work there, but they go down to Siraja every week-end so that the husband can go into the forest or do whatever he has to do there. To get to their house you turn off the main road (the famous Patia road) and go along a rather jungly track, and then there it is, right on the beach. It's a most attractive house, built on stilts, like many Thai houses, and painted white. It's enclosed in a sandy compound planted with flowering trees and one coconut palm by the gate, and lots of wooden seats in their shade. When we arrived Chirapa and her husband were waiting for us in the verandah part underneath the main house where there were more wooden and deck chairs and a dining table with room for six places.

We all took off our shoes and left them at the bottom of the stairs and then went up to the large, open sitting room, and Chirapa showed us our bedrooms. One of these was really a large landing between the other two but it could be shut off from the sitting room by a sliding door, and if we wanted to go through to the bathroom in the middle of the night while Warunee and her husband were asleep it was just too bad. Anyway, who cares at the seaside? The bathroom, of course, had no bath, but it had a tank filled with water and a dipper to throw water over yourself with, and it just sloshed over the floor and out through a hole in the corner. There was a wash-basin with a tap and the water came from large tanks with stored rainwater. They make their own electricity.

As soon as we were settled in we were given tea accompanied by Peak Frean biscuit puffs and marmalade from a brand new pot, presumably bought specially for the English visitors. They had brought two servants, a man and a woman, with them from Bangkok, and there was another local man whose normal job it was to look after the house when they were away, so we were well looked after. But Chirapa popped into the kitchen herself from time to time because Thai cooking needs a lot of preparation and a lot of supervision. She laid the table too (knowing the English way of doing it) but she didn't have to bother about serving or washing up. (Thais pay their servants a fantastically low sum, about 150 bahd a month, with all food thrown in. I reckon many more English people in England could afford servants at that rate!)

After tea we all packed into the Chirapa car (it's a bit awkward that I don't know her husband's name) and her husband drove us to see a large reservoir which has been made by damming up a valley. It looks rather odd because you can see the tops of trees growing out of the water, but the surrounding scenery was very beautiful, with tree-covered hills and large plantations of what I thought were bulrushes with white feathery top-nots, but it turned out to be sugar cane. It was all very nicely set out with roads and bridges, so that you could tour around and see all there was to see, and there was a sort of pavillion on a hill-top from which you could admire the view, and a 'government' rest house (closed). The reason for all this organised beauty was that it was planned by Pibulsonggram, the ex-prime-minister, and executed with public funds. In fact he was the only one who ever used the 'government' rest house and it hasn't been used since his deposition. Naturally he also enjoyed the amenities of the beautiful scenery and boating and fishing in and on the reservoir, but I think probably the public was also allowed to enjoy these when he wasn't there.

For dinner that night we had an enormous and delicious chicken pie which had been farmed out to a friend's cook who understood English tastes and was merely warmed up in the Chirapa oven. The pastry was as light as air and beautifully decorated and painted with egg white in the very best manner, and there were at least two meaty joints for each person, with a lavish helping of potatoes and peas. Everybody had two helpings and I was feeling comfortably satisfied when it was swept away (or what was left of it) and replaced by a Thai dish of curried chicken with chilli sauce. The Thais are very fond of chillis and all other hot things. No meal is complete without them, and, my goodness, they are hot. The servant came round and spooned enormous helpings of rice out of a silver bowl onto our plates, the chicken was dished out on top of it and mixed in. It was at this point during our stay that I first had a feeling of over-repletion which remained with me until at least 24 hours after our return to Bangkok.

After dinner we again got into the car and drove to Bangsaen, which is a seaside resort much used by Bangkok folk and consists mainly of rows of little wooden bungalows which you can hire for a couple of hours or a couple of nights or a couple of weeks, a hotel and several little eating shops. We cruised around for a bit and went along the pier, which was empty except for us and two fishermen, and then returned to the house. Warunee wanted to play vingt-et-un and win some money off Chirapa (Thais are great gamblers) but we said we wanted to go to bed so everybody else went to bed too. Not that we slept much. Thai beds are made of wooden boards with a thin kapok mattress an top and they're designed to make every limb of your body ache.

When I got up at half past seven next morning the Thais had all been up for a long time. Mr. Chirapa had taken Luen to Bangsaen and back in his speedboat but he offered to take me out for a trip and I was quite glad to go as I'd never been in a speedboat before. I thought we'd just flip round for ten minutes but he took me all the way to Bangsaen too and it took an hour to get there and back. Geoffrey says, rather bitterly, that he was just coming downstairs as we took off, and he never got a turn in the boat. My gosh, I never realised a speedboat could be so uncomfortable. If the sea's the least little bit rough, and if the boat goes too fast, you hit the water with great smacks and it's like hitting a solid surface with no give in it at all. Like a car with no springs. My whole body was jolted to bits to start with, and I prayed for the end of the journey, but after a while we slowed down, or the sea got smoother, I don't know which, and it was good fun. I quite wanted my breakfast when we got back, but once more there was too much to eat (fresh fish, fried egg left on the table to get cold, bread, butter and marmalade) and I felt very full again when we'd finished.

Our hosts were determined to entertain us to the full so that morning they took us to Siraja, to a new factory which is being built to make 'shaving board' out of wood shavings. It needs quite a lot of machinery for the process, but the result apparently is a hard, durable wood, which can be made to any size and is used mostly for making furniture. The machinery, newly arrived, was German and was being installed under the supervision of Germans, or German-speaking Swiss.

There was a chief-engineer in charge and a German chap looking after the machinery, both of whom we met. They were very enthusiastic and showed us everything. I got a bit bored but Geoffrey seemed quite interested, and Luen, who is rather a dull, colourless little man, grew quite animated over the electrical installations, because he's an electrical engineer.

After that we went into the saw mill, where it was Geoffrey's turn to grow animated because the wood was brought here by rail from the depth of the forest, and there were lots of funny little chuffa-trains sitting about, waiting to have their photographs taken (one of them with Geoffrey and me inside it). One of them even produced a little steam, but some of them were so old and delapidated that the scrap heap was their obvious destination, if there were such a thing in Thailand. It's a great country for leaving old and unwanted and disused and rubbishy things where they are (if there isn't a khlong handy to throw them into). This was the end of the morning's excursion and when we got back Geoffrey and I were very glad to go into the sea for a swim, but the other four didn't. For some reason Thai adults don't seem to think the sea is meant for swimming in, though children, and especially boys, love it. Lunch was curried chicken, rice, crabs, sweet-sour fish and one other amorphous dish (peppery hot, of course). At a Thai meal all the food is put on the table at the same time and you help yourself to the various dishes as you're ready. For this reason some of the food gets quite cold before you can get round to eating it. After this we had a rather dry swiss roll, obviously brought from Bangkok for Geoffrey's and my benefit. Oh dear! I nearly burst. Warunee is quite fat and looks as if she's used to eating a lot but

Luen is thin, yet I think he ate more than all of us. Chirapa, a slim type, rather pecked at her food and her husband didn't eat much because he said he had a delicate stomach. Probably from a long life of chilli-eating.

Well, at last there followed a long, decent pause for rest and recuperation, but as far as I was concerned it came too late. My tummy was complaining too much for sleep. At four o'clock we left with Warunee and Luen and we were home by six. Mind you, we had enjoyed ourselves enormously. We both said it, and we meant it. And the indigestion soon passed off. A day or two later Geoffrey was mouldy with aches and pains and a small temperature, but I think that was a kind of flu and nothing to do with chillis or crabs.

The rainy season has now passed away. The weather isn't much cooler but it's less humid and we can sleep at night without air-conditioning. Cocktail parties are much in vogue. People hire coloured lights for their gardens and you can drink your drinks on the lawn. The cricket season is about to begin and I'm beginning to think about my tennis racquet and golf clubs which I haven't used yet. The floods have all subsided, the lawns and tennis courts are dry, steam rollers are out repairing some of the damaged roads. In fact, in Thailand, winter is here.

Much love from Averin

6th December:
"A lot of diplomatic etiquette"

British Embassy,
Bangkok.

December 6th 1957

Dear Everybody,

Yesterday was the King of Thailand's birthday and a holiday for all government workers. A sort of Bank Holiday, in fact, but nothing like a Bank Holiday in England, when the shops are all shut and the streets in towns are rather dreary places. Here the shops were all open and eager to do business with people who don't usually get the opportunity to shop in the daytime. The only difference was that things looked a little more festive than usual, with flags flying and decorations out and one or two fairs in progress. We were out at nine o'clock in the evening to go to a cinema, and business was still brisk then. Shops, especially those in the Chinese area, were brightly lit and the streets were still thronged with people.

The king's birthday involves quite a lot of diplomatic etiquette. Yesterday Geoffrey had to put on his diplomatic uniform and go and sign the book and today he has to go with the ambassador and the counsellor and the military, air and naval attachés and the other first secretaries to pay his respects in the palace throne room. And on Sunday he dons diplomatic uniform for the third time for the Royal Garden Party, which I also have to attend in a long dress and long white gloves. This starts at about five o'clock in the evening and goes on for at least two hours, I'm told, so I hope there'll be some chairs for us to sit on, though I rather doubt if there will.

We celebrated the birthday yesterday with a late Sunday

morningish breakfast followed by sport at the Sports Club. Geoffrey had his second cricket net of the season and came away groaning, with a second bout of stiffness setting in. Meanwhile I had my first tennis game for two years and suffered no after effects at all. Why do our muscles react differently to unaccustomed exercise? Margaret, Stuart, this question is directed at you. After changing, Geoffrey staggered home to entertain work buddies to a drink while I had a swim, and for the first time since I've been here the water in the pool was cool enough to be refreshing. As John Patterson aptly remarked, it's usually like tepid green-pea soup. As I keep on telling you, winter is here. Yesterday the maximum temperature, at 5.10 pm., was 87.6° F. and the minimum at 6.10 a.m., 70.2° F. Still quoting from the newspaper, the average humidity was 81% which is very high by English standards, but quite comfortably low here.

We sent an enormous batch of Christmas cards off by bag last Tuesday. Nobody here has the slightest idea what it costs to send Christmas cards in England now, and anyway, none of us had anything but twopenny-halfpenny and halfpenny stamps, so we put twopenny-halfpenny ones on ours! I think it's rather dull to send cards from abroad without a foreign stamp and I feel sure some people will wonder how it's managed. The only one we're sending by airmail is the one to Mr. Primitt, our old gardener, who I'm sure would never believe that we were abroad if he didn't get a proper Thai stamp on his envelope. Anyway he said he collected stamps so a mere twopenny halfpenny one would not only mystify but disappoint him.

In a way it's difficult for us to realise that Christmas is near without the children to remind us, but there are signs and symptoms. We've been invited to a Christmas dinner on Christmas Eve and are planning to give some sort of a party ourselves, though I don't quite know when it will be. Yesterday I talked to a small girl of six who told me she had already written to Father Christmas and told him she wanted a doll and a rocking horse. I asked her how she managed to send the letter because there are no fireplaces in Bangkok, but she said it was quite simple. She went for a holiday in Malaya a short while ago (in the Cameron Highlands) and put her note up a chimney there! In the choir at Christ Church we are now practising carols to the exclusion of everything else, and about 20 odd bods have been roped in to swell our numbers. We practise two instead of one hours every Thursday evening and bellow ourselves hoarse over bits out of Handel's Messiah, as well as the usual carols. The choirmaster is an ex-choir-school boy and - he's a man now, of course - he carries us along with great gusts of enthusiasm, alternating with exasperation. The organist is a Chinese called Mr. See who isn't terribly quick off the mark and is apt to misunderstand his instructions so he comes in for a fair amount of the exasperation, and yesterday evening his difficulties were increased by a new bellows boy who sometimes failed to produce the necessary wind. "May we have the basses' note, Mr. See?" the choirmaster would say, and the organist would play the note, but nothing but a deep silence emerged. Then one or two people started drifting off to cocktail parties and this produced fresh waves of despair from Brian (the choirmaster). The main carol service is going to be on the Sunday evening before Christmas but I think we go round Carol singing to suitable listeners before that, and various people like the Rotary Club and the British Council ask us to perform, so life will be full of carols e'er long. Mr. Gilmour, the parson, and his wife, are naturally very busy with Nativity plays etc., but their task is made more difficult by the fact that the Bishop of Singapore is paying his annual visit just before Christmas. He stays with them and always uses Mrs. G. as his secretary, so what with that and the Bishop's Teaparty (a formidable-sounding function) and the other things they're both feeling rather desperate.

Much love from Averin

15th December:
"Such a lot of old crocks"

British Embassy,
Bangkok.

December 15th, 1957.

Dear Everybody,

This has been a week - well, eight days, really - with something happening every day, so if I ever get to the end of telling you about it this is going to be a long letter. However, it's Sunday efternoon and Geoffrey is playing cricket (temperatures, alas, up in the nineties again) so I've got a couple of hours or so before I go and take cup of tea with the team and see Geoffrey going in eleventh, or being hit for six, according to whether his side is batting or bowling.

Act I opens last Saturday afternoon, with me setting off to the hairdresser in order to have myself made smart for the King's birthday party next day. I choose a fairly quick hairdresser, and when they have finished with me (hair, fingers and toes) it isn't yet the time when Geoffrey said he might come and fetch me, so I decide to set off on foot to do my shopping. As I stroll along (it's foolish and conspicuous to hurry in Bangkok) a voice hails me in a recognisable language: "Hey, ma'am; can you tell us how to get to the British Club?" and I see two sailors across the street. I tell than I am going past the British Club and as we stroll together, I remember hearing of a ship in port, and I say brightly, "You're off Her Majesty's Ship Anzac, aren't you?". "H.M.I.S. Anzac," says one of the sailors, gently rebuking me. As we converse I am all the time wondering what the I stands for, and gradually their accent is borne in on me and I realise the I is an A and they are Australians. I go into the Club with them, meaning simply to show them the bar, but there I find one solitary Englishman, one Guy Beckitt, a

Liverpool man, the only British port adviser to the Thais, surrounded by Australians, entertaining them to Beer and Coca Cola. It is 4 o'clock to the afternoon, but he has obviously had no lunch and has been doing this worthy job since goodness knows what hour, so when he begs me beseechingly to stay and have a drink my heart melts and I perch on a stool, with a long cool grapefruit squash, and help him with idle prattle.

The scene now shifts to Geoffrey, who is wakened from his afternoon siesta with muddled thoughts of his wife and a hairdresser. She has told him which street the salon is in, so he drives there in the car, finds a suitable establishment, enquires within and is told that his wife will be ready in ten minutes. The British Club is just round the corner, so he goes there (goodness knows what for at 4 in the afternoon) and imagine his surprise when on entering the bar, he sees his wife whom he imagined to be one of those unrecognisable forms under a drier, perched on a stool, the only female in a sea of tarry males. He gives one blink of astonishment, then rallies with the self-control that only a diplomat can show and stands a drink all round. However, entertainment of gentlemen in uniform is excusable at all times so even afterwards, when we are alone on our shopping, his only comment is that he never, in his wildest dreams, imagined that one day he would come across his wife perched on a stool in a bar in Bangkok, surrounded by the Australian Navy. History doesn't relate what happened to the lady in the wrong beauty salon who was told her husband would be back for her in ten minutes ......

- no doubt she found some formula! (G.)

Act II finds the Hintons, on Sunday afternoon, doing up the last brass button on the diplomatic uniform and struggling into the almost shoulder-length chamois leather gloves which haven't been worn since Cairo days. Apart from the gloves Mrs. Hinton is wearing a long dress, a new dress which she has had made here and in which she feels rather good because (for once) her husband tells her he thinks she looks nice in it. At ten minutes past four they step into their car and are driven to the Royal Palace, where the King's Garden Party is to be held. It is still hot and the people who have already arrived are standing in groups shaped according to the long shadows of the few trees which grace the side of the garden to which we are directed. Presently a loud buzzer buzzes three times. Immediately the several thousand people stop talking, the heads of missions line up with their respective subordinates behind them, the path which forms a square round the garden is lined with these and myriads of Thai officials with their ladies, gorgeous in their many-coloured Thai silk dresses, and on the dot of five o'clock the king emerges from the palace, accompanied by the queen and a dozen court ladies and gentlemen. They walk slowly round the garden, the men bow, the ladies curtsey, and then, when the round is completed, everybody breaks rank and surges across the path, onto the central lawn, where tables laden with savoury sandwiches and sticky cakes and cups of tea or glasses of fruit cup await them. We are served by a few Palace servants, wearing white jackets and blue sort of skirty-trousery garments, and helped by boys of the king's school who wear white jackets, black shorts and long white socks. The royal pipe band strikes up with The Road to the Isles and everybody embarks on the age-old diplomatic game of making conversation with members of other nations. When the royal pipe band is tired the royal brass band takes its place, and these two worthy bodies jolly each other along throughout the whole long evening. Twilight comes and goes swiftly, and when it is dark coloured lights on the trees twinkle on and off, an illuminated fountain plays, every window in the palace is open and lit up, and opposite it the Government building is splendidly floodlit. Our feet, or our backs, or our tummies, ache with the long standing, but the talk must go on, and go on it does. Soon after 6.30 the king, a solemn young man of thirty, makes another tour of the garden, and the queen follows in his wake. The king reaches the end of his tour long before she does because she is far more friendly and stops here and there to talk. The king kicks his heels for a while, but at last he loses patience and goes back to look for her, and leads her at a smart pace to the end of the garden and on into the palace. It is exactly seven p.m. and the king's birthday party is over.

Contrary to the rules of the best dramatic productions, Act III is a comparatively short and insignificant one. It finds us on Monday evening entering the home of a Thai family, where Chewcheep, the beautiful British Council Librarian and her English husband, John Boyle, are holding their wedding reception. To them, of course, the occasion is an important one, but it marks the end of a long day, for they have already been married twice, once by the British Consul and once according to Thai customs. They are receiving their guests in Chewcheep's garden, which is lit with coloured lights and set with many chairs on which their guests, mercifully, may sit. We shake hands with the happy couple and proceed to the house, where we take off our shoes (no holes in your socks, I hope, gentlemen) and pay our respects in signs and muttered noises to the bride's mother. Out in the garden again we sit and chat to other British and English-speaking guests, drink coca cola or whisky, eat an enormous buffet supper of rice and fried and curried foods, grapple with the many insects that fall into our clothing, exhausted by their eternal dancing round the coloured lights, and finally withdraw at the decent hour of 9 p.m. It is at this hour that the oracle, faithfully consulted, has decreed that the guests should withdraw so that the older members of the family may carry on with the ceremony (deeply religious) of preparing the bed for the newly-married couple.

Act IV and Tuesday. This is the night of the Oxford and Cambridge Dinner. Black tie. 7.30 for dinner at 8 p.m. There are 78 men (a record) and 4 ladies (also a record), only one of whom is a Thai. We meet in an upper room in the British Club, where the tables are arranged in the shape of a square-ended W. Conversation is, of course, intellectual and animated though the dinner itself could have been better. The roast beef isn't bad, but Thai cooks evidently don't know how to cook Yorkshire pudding. When we have wined and dined Prince Prem, the chairman, rises and makes the first of his several witty speeches ('Your

Highnesses, Your Serene Highnesses, your Excellencies, Ladies and Gentlemen ...') and is followed by Mr. John Blofeld, writer and broadcaster for the B.B.C. who proposes the health of Oxford, with the usual witty (sometimes not very witty) jibes at the (to him) Other Place. John Blofeld has turned Buddhist and married a Chinese wife and I suspect that he has become so Easternised that he also takes opium. When I talked to him before dinner his eye-pupils were mere pin-points and his behaviour somewhat other-worldly. Next, H.E. Mr. Richard Whittington proposed the toast of Cambridge in a sometimes light and sometimes heavy manner and then His Highness Prince Vivadhanajai toasted the guests. His speech was a highly polished affair and very amusing, with some very close to the wind witticisms at the expense of the Prime Minister, Nai Pote Sarasin, and the American ambassador, Mr. Bishop, both of whom were present as guests. Pote Sarasin got his own back a bit when he proposed the toast of the hosts (he spoke remarkably good English even though he hadn't been to Oxford or Cambridge.) A gentleman called Nai Chaloke Komarakul na Nagara (whose name I defy you to pronounce) then made a speech toasting absent friends, and finally a young man called Watkins, obviously nursed by the Union, made us all laugh with a series of anecdotes in a speech which was supposed to be giving us the latest news of the Universities but left us with a very hazy notion of what was going on in either Oxford or Cambridge. So, with a brief compliment to

the four 'charming' members present (the ladies, I presume) Prince Prem wound all the Highnesses, Serene Highnesses, Excellencies, Ladies and Gentlemen up and we proceeded to the bar to listen to a tape-recording of the Oxford-Cambridge rugger match which had been being played while the dinner was in progress. The tape-recording was to take 45 minutes which seemed rather long to me so I wheedled the score out of the tape-recording man (who gave it to me only on the condition that I would then leave immediately and without communicating it to anyone else) and managed to persuade Geoffrey to come away with me, murmuring the sweet sounds Three-nil to Oxford gently in his ear.

On to Act V, and the present tense, out of which I seem inadvertently to have slipped .....

This consists of a buffet dinner for sixteen guests here on Wednesday evening, I think we can dispose of this occasion swiftly, with perhaps a brief mention of the fact that, since the rainy season is over, we ate at small tables out on the verandah, illuminated by little oil lamps which I had bought, after a long search, in the Chinese quarter, at 5 baht a piece, that afternoon. Guests included our Counsellor, Alec Adams, the Portuguese Chargé d'Affaires and his wife, a Danish couple, two Thai couples, a Thai odd man, a British Business couple, an ECAFE railway expert (British), a British vice-consul (a lady) and Arthur Maddox, First Secretary British Embassy. That doesn't add up to sixteen, so perhaps there were only fifteen guests after all.

Act VI finds us, on Thursday evening, at the house of D.J. Enright, poet, novelist and essayist, professor of English at Chulalongkhorn University. He is throwing a party in honour of Edmund Blunden who is his guest for two nights on his way back from leave in England to Tokyo, where he is Professor of English Literature. Edmund Blunden, as you may know, is a famous English poet, but to Geoffrey he spells Cricket, for when Geoffrey was at Worcester Edmund Blunden used to play against him in the Dean's Eleven. Edmund Blunden even had the grace to say he thinks he remembers Geoffrey.

I'm getting rather tired of this letter and I'm sure you are too. However, I must just mention briefly the Bishop of Singapore who has figured largely in the past two days. I think we'll abandon our dramatic form here. Shakespeare would be horrified, anyway, if he were confronted with a play with more than five acts.

The Bishop arrived on Friday with his wife and Geoffrey and I were asked to go and meet them at dinner at the parsonage that evening. It was another of these buffet dinners, and there were about a dozen of us there. The Bish was really very nice and his wife a nice friendly soul who had spent such an uncomfortable night on one of the hard parsonage beds that she said she simply must tackle the committee and get them to buy some new ones. Yesterday, the day of the Bishop's teaparty, the parsonage lawn was bedecked with brightly coloured coca cola umbrellas and tables and chairs. I went early in the afternoon to help prepare and worked really hard (for once, in this domesticated role), cutting cakes, arranging food on plates and, when the guests arrived, passing things round, and, when the guests departed, washing up. Everybody who ever goes to church was there, including our ambassador who hardly ever goes to church and looked rather sheepish. The parson's son, traditionally naughty, was there making a nuisance of himself and the whole thing passed off like any vicarage garden party on a summer afternoon. (Not that I've ever been to a vicarage garden party in England, but one can imagine these things).

Then again, this morning, I arose reluctantly at 8 o'clock, had breakfast, and left the house at five to nine (Geoffrey still in bed) to go to a choir practice for the morning service. Matins, complete with bishop, was at ten, and it sort of ran into a confirmation service, with the Bishop changing neck-bands surreptiously after the sermon, and two ushers setting out the Bishop's chair and a footstool discretely during the singing of a hymn. It was half-past eleven before all this was over, by which time Geoffrey, presumably, had been playing cricket for half-an-hour. He, of course, wants to hear the bishop preaching this evening, and I suppose I must go with him ....

But, talking of cricket, it's twenty to four and I'm already dying for a cup of tea, so if you'll excuse me I'll dash off to the Sports Club and see how things are going.

[Handwritten note to Margaret]

First cricket game of the season. I never saw such a lot of old crocks in my life. And Geoffrey's back was sunburnt through his shirt!

> *Much love, Averin*

P.S. When the children open the enclosed envelope, will you be so good as to divide the contents equally between them? It's for Christmas, of course.

NOTES

Ann, Michael and Jill all spent Christmas in Wallington, Surrey with Aunt Margaret, Uncle Stuart and cousins Ian, Carolyn and Vanessa. Averin and Geoffrey stayed in Bangkok and I'm sure had a whale of time with an unending but sadly undocumented round of cocktail parties and dinner parties.

27th December:
"Christmas day in the tropics"

British Embassy,
Bangkok.

December 27th, 1957.

Dear Everybody,

You'd think, wouldn't you, that with all you near and dear people miles away, Geoffrey and I would have a minimum amount of shopping to do at Christmas time, and yet we spent some very exhausting hours plodding round the shops during the few days before the 25th. There were friends and friends' children to be disposed of, and servants and servants' children, and Thai work acquaintances (even the wheels of diplomacy have to be oiled sometimes), not to mention ourselves. And every gift had to be haggled over and bargained for, which added to the purchase time of each one. Several tempers were lost during these expeditions, but fortunately they were soon found again. To add to the general discomfort it was very hot work, and the cheapest shops are in the smelliest districts so there was that too, so what with one thing and another it was a happy time when Christmas Day arrived and the shoppings were all over.

I suppose we started celebrating on Christmas Eve, when we went out to dinner with the Pattersons. There were eight of us altogether, all Embassy people, so for once we could dispense with sparkling conversation and relax. John and Anne played us suitable Christmas music on gramophone records, and we all sat and said very little, all being rather hot and exhausted and presently we ate turkey (a dessicated turkey imported from America via Singapore, a rather small bird, and, frankly, one had to exert one's imagination pretty hard to realise that it was a turkey at all). John, who is only 24, had never carved anything before and it rather fell to pieces at his touch, but in spite of all these unfavourable circumstances we all enjoyed it very much. Then came Christmas pudding (tinned, imported, but very good), and after that we all felt pretty full and conversation lapsed even more. However, Mildred Forrester, a 2nd Secretary and vice-consul, a rather stout and plain but supremely kind-hearted lady in her middle-forties, had brought with her her first cinematographic essays together with a projector, and she entertained us for half an hour with various shots of visits to temples and familiar colleagues splashing about the embassy compound when it was flooded, either in cars or in wellingtons, or bare-foot. There was the distinct mark of the amateur about these films. There were long gaps when nothing seemed to appear at all, and sometimes misty scenes would flicker onto the screen, then quickly fade away, and sometimes we had exciting, magnified visions of Mildred's own face which she had somehow managed to 'shoot' sideways on, presumably when she was gazing into the works to see if something was wrong. However, it was all good fun, and we were supremely grateful to her for entertaining us in this way.

Then at last five of us set off to midnight communion. This is something Geoffrey and I had never done before, but Anne, Mildred and I were all singing in the choir and John and Geoffrey perforce came along too. If you're trying to picture the scene you must remember that it was hot, even at midnight. The men were wearing shirts and ties but no jackets and we choir ladies took off our dresses and put on blue skirts and surplices (or whatever you call the white, shapeless, blousy things that choristers wear) and still felt pretty warm. Believe me, the idea of bleak midwinter and snow on snow was pretty hard to conjure up. The church was all lit up and a gramophone record of church bells playing carols was amplified from the top of the tower (there are no real bells there, as far as I know). The choir all gathered on the grass outside at the west end and we processed up the aisle singing Once in Royal David's City, and at the end of the service, out in the porch, we sang the first two carols of Christmas morning. There was a large

Christmas tree in the church with tinselly decorations, but no nativity scene, which I rather missed.

On Christmas morning, with no stocking-eager children to wake us up, Geoffrey and I slept late and were only just alert and breakfasted in time to be back in church at 10 for the Christmas morning service. More choir singing, of course, with more 'Unto us' and the 'Hallelujah Chorus', which the choir didn't really want to do again, only the choir master was so pleased with the first attempt at the carol service that he was determined to get in a repeat performance. And then we went for a drink, with many other people and their children, on the lawn outside the Counsellor's house, in the Embassy Compound. H.E was there in a blue short-sleeved shirt and flannels and Mrs. Whittington, somewhat smarter, having just come from the R.C. church, and most of the Embassy staff and various other bods. And while we drank the W.T. man handed Geoffrey two telegrams, one signed Hinton Stephen Macalister and the other from the Jameses in Hatfield, which was all very exciting. And than Geoffrey and I went home for lunch, and then, at last, we - no we didn't. I've missed something out.

No, before lunch we called all the servants into the sitting room and they came in their best clothes, Suk looking terribly smart in a long-sleeved white shirt and long, neatly creased trousers, Cooky with a clean shirt on, and Wirart's children dressed up in party clothes. We sat them down and I pretended to be number one boy and passed round coca cola and green spot (a fizzy orange drink) and beer which Geoffrey dispensed from the frig.-bar. Conversation rather languished as our Thai is not yet suitable for talking fluently, and we addressed remarks in English to those who could speak it and they translated it for those who couldn't. And then Geoffrey doled out presents, money for the money-earners, a book for Som See and toys for the children and then they all melted away and then we had our solitary lunch.

After that we gathered round, Geoffrey and I, and opened

our presents. Do you picture us a rather pathetic couple, with only two-and-a-half parcels between us, spinning out the untying of each knot, and lingering over the unfurling of each piece of brown and pretty paper? If so, you must picture again because we had a quite fantastic number of presents from Thai friends (wheels of diplomacy, again, and also all my pupils made their contribution), and as shops in Bangkok make a habit of wrapping gifts up in coloured paper and tying them with coloured ribbon, finished-off with an elaborate bow, by the time we'd finished the floor was as littered as a tree-ceremony floor at home. Naturally your presents were opened first, and we cooed happily over the photograph album and stick-in corners, the cigarette lighter and refill, the razor and razor towel, the tobacco, the diaries and Jilly's calendar, but after that - well, there were guest towels and hankies, china ornaments, a silver bowl with orchids, Thai silk scarves, dinner mats, a gold brooch, preserved ginger and Turkish delight ..... Really, that half-hour after lunch was a very happy time.

After that came siesta time, and while the Hintons are busy sleeping perhaps I should tell you that we had made the sitting-room quite gay with our many Christmas cards hung round the walls on ribbons and little Chinesey-lanterny dangly things which Geoffrey had laboriously pinned up on the cross beams one evening a few days before Christmas. And we had one huge coloured paper ball, bought from the commissary and much admired by Som See. In the evening Chirapa and her husband, Pradit, and Warunee and Luen came to dinner and we gave them fish cooked in the Thai way in sweet-sour sauce, followed by roast duck and green peas, followed by Christmas pudding and mince pie, which they obviously didn't like much but they took small helpings and plodded nobly through most of it, followed by fruit. Then we made them pull crackers and they sat solemnly for the rest of the evening in paper hats, probably thinking this was an odd thing to do, but one must humour the English during their Christmas celebrations.

So that was Christmas day in the tropics, and the next day

was a holiday so we took a picnic lunch and drove furiously for two-and-a-half hours to look for, and eventually find, a much spoken of water-fall, which turned out to be only about 6 feet high! However, it was in pleasant surroundings, with little wooden tables and benches where visitors could sit and eat, and a flower garden, and all of it free, unlike similar pleasure resorts in England. Part of the way there was along a road called Friendship Highway which was built by the Americans and is a most remarkable (for Thailand) achievement. For the first time since we've been here Geoffrey was able to drive consistently at 80 miles an hour and the car was quite superb, with no tremor or sign of effort. It was in very lovely country, among wooded, craggy hills, and the trees were green and autumn shades of orange and pink and brown. In a way, it's odd to experience autumn without the customary nip in the air, but very nice to see the varied colours for a change.

And now the scene has faded out and faded in again to Sunday afternoon, and Geoffrey is playing cricket but I have no resentful feelings as I had my sportive fling at an early hour this morning. After a fleeting tussle with my conscience I decided to skip church, having had an overdose of it during the past week, and at 9.30 I went to play tennis with Eban Evans of the British Council. He hadn't played for six years and I hadn't played properly for two and we both wanted to try ourselves out, and he beat me 6-0, 6-2, but it was good fun and I gave him enough of a game for him to enjoy it. It was terribly hot and I felt quite limp towards the end, but afterwards I went to the Sports Club and had a swim and that was very delicious. In the meantime Geoffrey went to church on his own and evidently other people besides me had played truant because there was no choir at all!

Yesterday we had wonderful letters from everybody, Dai (Florence had written during the week before), Mummy, Margaret, Michael and Jill. There was Ann's excellent school report, which revealed that although the average age in her class is 12.5 she is only 11.7, and Michael told us about his two prizes for maths and

English, and Jill said that Mrs. Tomlinson had told her her report was good (it hasn't reached us yet), so really, if you'll forgive me saying so, we are terribly pleased and proud.

I've a horrid feeling our Christmas presents won't have reached you in time, and if they do come they will have lost their significance. But if they don't arrive at all I shall make protests this end. I have, after all, a receipt.

[Handwritten note to Margaret]

Very, <u>very</u> many thanks to you and Stuart for your many kindnesses to the children at Christmas, and the presents you and all the family gave them. You've no idea (or have you?) what a relief it is to know that they were - are - happy and kindly looked after, & I hope to goodness the effort hasn't exhausted you. How on earth did you find time to write a letter on the 22nd, & prod Michael into writing one?

Thank you very much for the diary & calendar, both of which will be invaluable. Do you <u>really</u> want to give us another present? We feel strongly that you've dispensed enough generosity by looking after Michael & having the girls for Christmas. As a matter of fact we can see any number of magazines here, because the Embassy & the British Council both take in most of the best ones. I already have a subscription to Argosy, and as a matter of fact the only one that is <u>really</u> missing from the picture is the Railway Magazine, which G. would <u>love</u> to have! I'd like him to have it too, just to keep him happier. It costs 2/6 monthly.

A happy, successful New Year to all of you --

Much love from Averin.

Acknowledgements

These letters are published in memory of my mother and father, Averin and Geoffrey Hinton.

Many thanks to my son John Hinton and my sister Ann Anley for transcribing the majority of the letters, for reading and commenting and generally being very helpful.

<u>Photographs</u>

Cover Wat Ratchanatdaram (monochrome): Z3144228 / CC BY-SA (https://creativecommons.org/licenses/by-sa/4.0)

Cover Royal barge (cropped): Lerdsuwa / CC BY-SA (https://creativecommons.org/licenses/by-sa/3.0)

Cover Averin & Geoffrey at Bang Pa-In, © Michael Richard Hinton

Foreword Averin and Geoffrey in St Albans, spring 1957, © Michael Richard Hinton

25th May 1957 M.S. Oranje poster: 1950s poster, copyright holder unknown

1st June 1957 Samlor-filled street in the 1950s: public domain

1st June 1957 The house at 46 Soi Lang Suan, Bangkok, © Michael Richard Hinton

5th June 1957 Som See and Chai, No.1 boy and her mother, © Michael Richard Hinton

5th June 1957 Suk the gardener, © Michael Richard Hinton

11th June 1957 Wat Benchamabophit: BerryJ / CC BY-SA (https://creativecommons.org/licenses/by-sa/4.0)

11th June 1957 Monks and Buddha in Phutthamonthon: ผู้สร้างสรรค์ผลงาน/ส่งข้อมูลเก็บในคลังข้อมูลเสรีวิกิมีเดียคอมมอนส์ - เทวประภาส มากคล้าย / CC BY-SA (htts://creativecommons.org/licenses/by-sa/2.5)

Menu for a Chinese meal General Phao: public domain

11th June 1957 (2) Golden mount Wat Saket: Ahoerstemeier / CC BY-SA (https://creativecommons.org/licenses/by-sa/3.0/)

13th June 1957   Guests at the Queen's birthday party, © Michael Richard Hinton

Train Journey to Songkla   Express train at Bangkok station 1950s, © Michael Richard Hinton

2nd July 1957   Ann, Michael & Jill in St Albans, 1957, © Michael Richard Hinton

2nd July 1957   Averin teaching English, © Michael Richard Hinton

16th July 1957   Ruins at Ayuthia: Patricia Young / Public domain

23rd July 1957   Phra Pathom Chedi: Preecha.MJ / CC BY-SA (https://creativecommons.org/licenses/by-sa/4.0)

5th August 1957   Averin & Geoffrey at Bang Pa-In, © Michael Richard Hinton

19th August 1957   Chungkai war cemetry at Kanburi (Kanchanaburi) x 2 photos, © Michael Richard Hinton

19th August 1957   Ngo Dinh Diem, president of Vietnam: public domain

2nd September 1957   Sightseeing with group including Geoffrey and policeman from Singapore, © Michael Richard Hinton

9th September 1957   Geoffrey in uniform for the Ambassador's presentation to the King, © Michael Richard Hinton

9th September 1957   Embassy male staff on the Palace steps, © Michael Richard Hinton

16th September 1957   Part of War-Graves cemetry at Chungkai, © Michael Richard Hinton

23rd September 1957   Prime Minister Pibulsonggram, General Phao and Field Marshal Sarit: public domain

14th October 1957   Spirit house in the garden at 46 Soi Lang Suan, © Michael Richard Hinton

About Averin Hinton   Photo of Averin Hinton, © Michael Richard Hinton

With apologies if any errors have been made in these attributions. Please notify the publisher of any errors, and we will make sure we rectify them.

books@orrydian.co.uk

About Averin Hinton

Averin was born in Liverpool in 1921. Her father, Dr Charles Macalister, was a consultant physician and paediatrician at various Liverpool hospitals. He was in his late 50s when Averin was born and already had six children from a previous marriage, some of whom were older than his second wife Leslie. Averin writes in her memoirs of the difficulties she and her mother and her sister Margaret experienced at the hands of the half-siblings, who weren't at all keen on their father indulging in a new family and thereby diluting their inheritance.

Averin studied at Cheltenham Ladies College and then in the early war years read Modern Languages at Somerville College, Oxford. There, in 1941, she met Geoffrey Hinton on a punt on the River Cherwell, and they married the following year. He was immediately posted to Egypt to work as an intelligence officer, while she stayed at Oxford to complete her degree and then went to work in London for SIS, the Secret Intelligence Service, for the remainder of the war.

Geoffrey died in 1980, very soon after taking retirement, and Averin died in 2005. She often expressed a wish that these letters should be published, along with her memoirs, which describe her life up to her first meeting with Geoffrey.

Titles available in this series

Averin's Letters from Bangkok, Part 1: 1957
ISBN 978-1-8382489-3-2

Averin's Letters from Bangkok, Part 2: 1958.
ISBN 978-1-8382489-4-9

Averin's Letters from Bangkok, Part 3: 1959-1961
ISBN 978-1-8382489-5-6

Averin's War: Letters home from Oxford and London 1940-1944
ISBN 978-1-8382489-9-4

books@orrydian.co.uk

CPSIA information can be obtained
at www.ICGtesting.com
Printed in the USA
LVHW011420160821
695421LV00025B/2029